Dialoguing with Critical Race Theory

Constitutional and Christian Links

Mark Ellingsen

Series Editor

Leland Harper

Siena Heights University

Series in Philosophy of Race

VERNON PRESS

www.vernonpress.com

In the Americas:
Vernon Press
1000 N West Street, Suite 1200
Wilmington, Delaware, 19801
United States

In the rest of the world:
Vernon Press
C/Sancti Espiritu 17,
Malaga, 29006
Spain

Series in Philosophy of Race

Library of Congress Control Number: 2024939351

ISBN: 979-8-8819-0140-0

Also available: 978-1-64889-896-9 [Hardback]; 979-8-8819-0051-9 [PDF, E-Book]

Cover design by Vernon Press with elements from Freepik.

For the heritage and liberating mission of the Interdenominational Theological Center.

Table of Contents

Acknowledgments

This dedication is really to a community, to the Black community and its courage, creativity and leadership. I've been a fan. These words are written

> In hopes that together we might make it the day when King's Dream, DuBois' vision of the Awakening of the vigor of Black souls sweeping irresistibly toward the Goal, and even the realization of Bell's conviction that the Something Real for Black people is not far off.

Chapter 1

Critical Race Theory: What Americans Are Saying About It

Want to pick a fight with someone? Mention Critical Race Theory, and there is a chance you can get into an argument, especially if your partner is of a different race, different social class, or different educational background. If you have different understandings of what the Civil Rights Movement achieved, you and your partner are also likely to squabble over CRT. Critical Race Theory (CRT) is a cross-disciplinary approach used by lawyers, sociologists, and civil rights activists to explain how to do something about the fact that laws, socio-political institutions (including educational institutions), and media shape and are shaped by conceptions of race and ethnicity. One of its goals is to challenge the prevailing notions of racism and racial justice. It has been linked in pop culture to The 1619 Project, a journalistic endeavor developed by *New York Times* writers to reframe U.S. history by placing the consequences of slavery at the center of the nation's national narrative. Some contend that Critical Race Theory is a creation of the political Right or of the media. But the next chapter will quickly dispatch that nonsense as we examine the theory's origins in the upper echelons of legal scholarship.

Before 1993 the term "Critical Race Theory" received no attention in the general public. Indeed, the movement was just being developed, but that year, it surfaced when Bill Clinton's nominee Lani Guinier as Assistant Attorney General for Civil Rights was stifled when Guinier was identified with Critical Race Theory.

In 2010 the developed theory got some press coverage when a primer on CRT was banned from Tucson, Arizona, schools as a result of a state law forbidding race-conscious education in Arizona public schools. (The law was later deemed unconstitutional.) But CRT really owes its pop-culture renown to Donald Trump! In both the run-up to the 2020 Presidential election and its aftermath, Trump and conservative commentators made opposition to Critical Race Theory a significant campaign theme. He expressly denounced it in a September 17, 2020 speech, and during that month, he also issued an executive order directing all agencies of the federal government to cease funding of all programs that mention white privilege or Critical Race Theory (see the 2020 memorandum written on behalf of the President by Russell Vaught). The agenda of these programs was said to be divisive, un-American, and racist. To that list, a lot of Evangelical Christians have added that CRT is un-Christian.

Conservative organizations, their think tanks like the Heritage Foundation, American Legislative Exchange Council, and most anything the Koch brothers subsidize, as well as conservative media have continued the critique of CRT. There is a lot at stake for conservatives, especially according to Sociologist Carol Swain. She notes in *Black Eye for America* (p.55) that CRT has significantly impacted both the media and the academy. Brookings Institute reported that in the final months of 2021, it was mentioned 13,000 times on Fox News. It is perhaps receiving a little less attention in conservative media today. For as of early 2024, 18 States had banned the teaching of Critical Race Theory in their schools. It has become the bogeyman for those unwilling to acknowledge our nation's racist history and its continuing effects, or a code phrase to this constituency for any person or idea who wants to contend that systemic racism and injustice are still issues to address today in America. There is evidence that these developments have been deliberate, as a quote from a leader of the anti-Critical Race Theory Movement Christopher Rufo notes the critics' strategies:

> We have successfully frozen their brain – "critical race theory" – into the public conversation and are steadily driving up negative perceptions. We will eventually turn it toxic, as we put all of the various cultural insanities under that brand category... The goal is to have the public read something crazy in the newspaper and immediately think "critical race theory." We have decodifiedthe term and will recodify it to annex the entire range of cultural constructions that are unpopular with Americans. (reported by Meckler and Dawsey)

Numerous books against CRT written by conservatives have appeared, including *Cynical Theories* (in 2020) by Helen Pluckrose and James Lindsay, as well as *Fault Lines* (2021) by Voddie Baucham and *Irresistible Revolution* (also in 2021) by Matthew Lohmeier. In accord with Rufo's strategies, a conservative expert in Educational Theory, Jonathan Butcher (*Splintered*, pp.208-212) has even contended that Critical Race Theory is taught in American schools today. (But he points out only a few such schools, and makes his point by identifying schools claiming all institutions are racist as CRT, a bit of a stretch as we will observe.)

There is evidence that these dynamics explain or are at least related to the ever-growing number of States and local school boards (under Republican domination) which are banning CRT in their educational systems. At last report educational gag orders inhibiting the teaching of any race theory (including Critical Race Theory) in state schools and universities had been filed in 9 State Legislatures in addition to the 18 which already have laws to this effect on the books. It is little wonder that anger about these actions would be articulated in segments of the Black community, as the NAACP has condemned such actions for effectively denying students glimpses of slavery and oppression as viewed from a Black perspective. Don't these sentiments make sense?

Why all the furor from the Right? Conservative scholar Carol Swain and her co-author Mark Schorr claim that Critical Race Theory pits "the people" against "elites" (p.60). The conservative think tank Heritage Foundation and the Moms for America organization well express reasons for the backlash. Critical Race Theory is said to be rooted in Marxism, substituting "racial groups" for "economic classes" as what drives history and economics (Swain and Schorr, esp. pp. 13,17,21ff.; Butcher, pp.168-169,208,262). Swain and Schorr go so far as even to label CRT as itself racist (pp.,18; cf. Butcher, pp.44ff.).

CRT is said incorrectly to make race the prism through which proponents analyze all aspects of American life (much like the 1619 Project has). In so doing, it contributes to division in America. As such, the theory promotes both explicit racism (Black against white) and racial guilt in white children (especially with its idea of implicit biases and calls for white students to "renounce their whiteness"). Swain and Schorr (p.50) contend that this is a violation of the Constitution's 14th Amendment and its protection of the learning environment from hostilities on the basis of race. In fact, according to Carol Swain (January 9, 2020; January 15, 2020; January 22, 2020), CRT posits that the experience of people from marginalized groups has more weight than the experience of mainstreamed (white groups). Swain and her colleague Christopher Schorr (p.15) also lament that CRT will not allow any Black-white collaboration unless both parties benefit.

Conservative Educational theorist Jonathan Butcher (*Splintered*, pp.17-18,102-106) contends that several pro-CRT state public-school and private school curricula design coursework that does not consider America as a land of opportunity in which we are all Americans, but rather portray us as members of different tribes, competing for power. College campuses also host CRT commitments (Butcher, pp.119-160). Indeed, Swain and her co-author (p.29) cite numerous examples of how CRT's implementation in our schools effectively demeans white students. For example, in Illinois, 7th and 8th grade students were told to remain silent and lower their eyes (a gesture of submission) while being taught by their CRT instructor. In New York, white employees were instructed that their racial identity is "toxicity in the air."

Jonathan Butcher (pp.68-70,76) contends that even the development of new Math techniques which intersperse mathematical instruction with instruction on social responsibility and critiques of capitalist imperialism (so-called Equitable Math) is a child of Critical Race Theory. Butcher (pp.107ff.) also notes how Critical Race Theory suppositions have impacted Anti-bias Training, which has itself become a big business, garnering over $8 billion a year from businesses employing these services. His hypotheses and the actions of school districts against Critical Race Theory are all the more baffling insofar as CRT is not just one thing. In fact, we'll note that it is more a movement endorsing some common themes, but also reflects a fair share of diversity among its proponents.

In the case of some Evangelical Christian critics, the points we have just noted lead to the charge of CRT's un-Christian character, for it is overlooking the possibility and power of redemption (Swain and Schorr, pp.40-41). It also is said to undermine the Christian belief in the unity of all people (*Ibid.*, p.74). Rather than advocate Christian principles of love of the neighbor, it is alleged that CRT is rooted in conflict and the perpetual search for enemies, oppressors, and victims (Butcher, pp.176,188ff.). In addition, Swain and Schorr (pp.10-11) contend that CRT confers godlike characteristics on whites, as all that happens to Blacks is understood as the creation of every malady Blacks face. They also contend that anti-racism has become a new religion (pp.44-45). As Evangelicals, Swain and Schorr also contend that mainline Protestantism has been coopted by CRT (p.57).

Critical Race Theory is said by its critics to seek to end discrimination by discriminating (Swain and Schorr, pp.52-53; see this affirmation by Ibram Kendi in *Summary: How To Be an Antiracist*, pp.18-19). Educational theorist Jonathan Butcher (p.26) observes that CRT is undertaking efforts to have children learn to treat people based on the color of their skin. Benjamin Carson ("Foreward," *Black Eye for America*, p.xv) who served in the Trump administration has chimed in on these points and blamed CRT for contributing to the present polarization which characterizes American society. Carol Swain (*Black Eye for America*, p.1) contends that CRT has spawned the "cancel culture" as well as racially segregated dormitories on college campuses. She also contends that CRT rejects science, reason, and objectivity as "white" (p.18). According to Jonathan Butcher (pp.144,205), genuine communication is precluded by CRT and its commitment to subjectivity and perspectival interpretation of everything said or written. As we have noted, these allegations entail the charge that CRT challenges the values of classic liberalism (*Black Eye for America*, pp.30-31; Butcher, p.165).

A further critique of CRT emerges from its practitioners' claim that all acts of the white majority entail racism. It is argued against this possibly valid point that if Blacks were so delicate to take offense and suffer trauma from microaggressions, that in itself is denigrating to African Americans (Butcher, p.155).

It is not surprising then that critics also allege that CRT claims regarding America and its Constitution being rooted in white privilege aim at undermining patriotism and the American Dream (Butcher, pp.27,51,166,180-181). The CRT claims that racism can never be overcome and its corresponding belief that white efforts to fight racism are driven by self-interest challenge the American founding ideals about freedom and equality under law. Challenges are also issued to CRT by contending that it posits systems in America which allegedly do not allow non-whites to succeed. This can readily enhance defeatism among African Americans, it is alleged, undermining their desire to achieve.

The Legal Insurrection Foundation, a conservative nonprofit organization, contends that in virtue of its insistence that all ideas and texts must be examined in relation to their use in their social context and the intention of their authors, CRT challenges the very foundations of our liberal order, as it questions rationalism, individualism, Constitutional law, and legal reasoning (see Swain and Schorr, pp.30-31). But what is overlooked in that critique and in others which follow is that these alleged traits of CRT are not idiosyncratic to the theory, but tend to dominate in the academy in most Humanities and Social Scientific disciplines (see Allan Bloom, *The Closing of the American Mind*). Why ban CRT and not such "white" versions of these critiques? Such observations lead Educational Theorist Jonathan Butcher (pp.56-58) along with colleagues like Maria Ledesma (and Dolores Caldéron, *Qualitative Inquiry* 21, No.3 [March 2015]) as well as Gloria Ladson-Billings (*International Journal of Qualitative Studies in Education*, 11, No.1 [January 1998]: 7-24) to conclude that CRT's suppositions have taken over our educational system as well as the academy. And a January 20, 2021, Executive Order by Joe Biden titled "Advancing racial Equality and Support for Underserved Communities through the Federal Government" supported this position by calling on teachers to focus on racist acts and systems in the American past.

Some legal scholars also critique the movement for its emphasis on storytelling, which is viewed as ineffective and analytically unsound (Richard Posner, *The Problems of Jurisprudence*; Susanna Sherry and Daniel Farber, *Beyond All Reason: The Radical Assault on Truth in American Law*). Another problem that is noted by critics is that proponents of the theory seem not to promote blueprints for the improvement, saying nothing more than offering a few policies and then suggesting that we wait to see if such policies improve things (Butcher, pp.159-170). But of course our Constitutional system seems to operate this way.

The Right's attacks on CRT in the public school system and in society as a whole have been met with resistance from the Left, notably by the American Association of University Professors, The National Education Association, and various teachers' unions. (But these actions certainly do not guarantee the presence of CRT in all our schools, as voices on the Right seem to allege.) This has in turn entailed that the critique of CRT is an occasion for critiques of every organization and movement perceived as "woke" or opposed to the free market, and of course, Fox News, with the assistance of Facebook and Twitter, will do all they can to contribute to making the debate even more fierce.

It is debatable whether this debate in its present form is good for America. Certainly, the vitriol and anger of the debate is not in the interests of national unity. And when we look at what it is doing to our public schools (and perhaps university life) it does not seem that the debate best serves American interests. If you teach in a school or serve on a state university faculty (no matter what your job), when you encounter touchy, controversial subjects, the wisest thing to do is dodge them. Nowhere is this better illustrated than in how the State of Georgia has dealt with the CRT controversy in its public school system. A June 3, 2021, Resolution of the Georgia State Board of Education in resolving that no school district shall teach "an individual, by virtue of his or her race or sex, is inherently racist" or that "an individual, by virtue of his or her race or sex, bears responsibility for actions committed in the past" (clear shots at CRT), "believes no teacher... shall be compelled... to discuss current events..." In short, part of not teaching CRT is that current events are optional! And even in States that do not go this far, human nature and our natural self-protectiveness is going to tilt teachers away from controversial subjects about race and sex in a school banning CRT, and the best way to do that is not to teach present controversies. Do we really want to put an end to current events education in our schools?

Next Steps in Creating a Dialogue

For all the reasons just noted as well as the public's lack of understanding of Critical Race Theory (some even think it is just a media creation), we need a book like this one. If we are going to dialogue with Critical Race Theory, we first have to know what it is and what it really teaches (cut through and around all the myths). That is what we are up to in the next chapter. We will see that CRT is first and foremost an academic legal theory. It is not the work of a bunch of anti-intellectual activists. It may have some faint links to Marxism and even at points use the insights of Marxism, but it did not emerge out of Communism. Indeed, it has very European Enlightenment suppositions. We'll see that it is not un-American, at least not in its origins. We will also explore some of its controversial teachings and how it seems critical of Constitutional system and some religious convictions. In addition, I'll close with some data that will make you wonder if perhaps there is some validity to CRT claims about the structural racism of American institutions. And if that data does not convince you, at least it will get you thinking about what data you can produce to undermine the claims CRT makes.

In this spirit of trying to facilitate a real dialogue with and not harangues against Critical Race Theory, the third chapter explores CRT's dialogue with the American Constitution. We'll explore the validity of some of the CRT critiques of our Constitutional system, both its original failure to outlaw slavery and the way in which it has been implemented even after post-Civil War and LBJ Great Society amendments. But I think that along with no less than the great Abolitionist Frederick Douglass, a case is made for contending that the majority of the Founders and government system they created were biased towards ending the slave trade, ensuring the protection of the life and welfare of African-Americans, as well as protecting the welfare of all who are impoverished. Through an analysis of *The Federalist Papers,* I will show that the Founders operated with a realism about factions, a belief that those with power will do what it takes to maintain power. It is noted that the optimistic Jeffersonian strand of the American political system has largely silenced this realistic theme in American society and our politics. The chapter probes how these insights link with Critical Race Theory's pessimism about liberal politics and how the system coerces minorities into certain behaviors. These insights will make us more self-critical, prompt us always to question even the best laws and policies to ensure that they do not benefit those in power to the detriment of everyone else. The Founders' intentions to curtail factions by means of the separation of powers instituted by the Constitution offer possible resources for fighting racism, contesting the "normalization" of whiteness, and overcoming American forgetfulness about the plight of the poor.

Of course, present political dynamics (the system's domination by the rich) need to be considered as reasons why racism and systems favoring whites remain in place. The Founders' appeals to common sense are examined as a way of addressing these abuses. And I will make the case that this orientation effectively challenges the separatist and subjectivist propensities of Critical Race Theory, a critique I do want to make of CRT. The point of the chapter, though, is to demonstrate that if you do not want to teach Critical Race Theory in our schools due to its un-American suppositions, better not teach the Constitution either. The two share that many common suppositions.

Many of the same intentions guide my thinking in Chapter Four. In the previous chapter, we will examine how indebted the Founders were to the Christian doctrine of Original Sin (St. Augustine's version) in developing their view of factions and the imperfect character of our political system. After reviewing the doctrine of Original Sin and its origins, it will become obvious how the view of human nature of the Founders (including Madison and Hamilton) is indebted to Christian thinking on that point. We are all indeed self-interested selfish "sons-of-guns," concupiscent women and men always seeking pleasure. This insight should vindicate African American perceptions of structural racism and take some of the edge off critiques for whites about the conclusion of Critical Race Theory that "all whites are racists." Christianity teaches that white people, indeed all of us, always seek our own self-interest.

Christian insights help us further to live and work with the supposition that our institutions and laws always require vigilance.

Christian faith also has some answers to the mess we are in. Although church structures have too infrequently embodied this faith commitment, the Christian Word of God teaches that ultimately ethnic differences do not matter. Critical Race Theory's insights about the fact that racial differences are more about social condition than genetics are vindicated. Insights from Biology and the Human Genome Project in particular support this insight. Modern insights from the field of Evolution are also found to support this sense of human harmony as new research suggests that the human cooperative propensities are what account for the success of the human race. Of course, something like that has been taught for nearly 2 millennia by the Christian faith. The Christian and Evolutionary belief that we can discern a common morality represents an amendment of Critical Race Theory's position, which might render it more effective in accomplishing its aims as it gains broader public support. Christian insights (especially the call to appeal to a common morality [natural law] like America's Founders did, along with the hopefulness about the future the Christian faith brings) might offer a model for building the sort of coalitions it will take to overcome racism in American society. In view of the largely overlooked overlaps between CRT and Christian faith, it seems again that the Right must consider the consequences of seeking to bar instruction in our schools of the perspectives of Critical Race Theory. Ban them, and be sure never to teach in a descriptive way how Christian suppositions have shaped American society. If they coincide with CRT, exposing the young to such teaching must be terminated. Of course, the Evangelical Right will not want to do that.

In the final segment, the book concludes by raising the question again of whether Critical Race Theory is not really as American and wholesome as the Constitution and Christian faith. If we get to that stage, we might begin to remove a lot of the nastiness among Americans that's been rising to the surface and not allowed real debate. But this conclusion cautions that we not stop there. Although we want to avoid separatism, I'll make the case that there is something very correct about the theory's supposition that we need to ensure that Black autonomy in overcoming racism is heeded, that the oppressed know best what they need, should define it themselves, and that unless we are ever vigilant, white leadership in fighting racism can easily evolve into a movement which serves white interests. (Christianity and the Constitution teach us that too.) Then the book aims to get very practical, closing with an examination of the next steps, how embracing the insights of Critical Race Theory in synthesis with the best strands of our Constitutional system and Christian faith could change America and race relations. A few of the many proposals outlined in my book *Wired for Racism?* and also those particular proposals emerging from

Critical Race Theory will be sketched briefly regarding access to votes, getting big money out of politics, Affirmative Action, reparations, a media which no longer make "whiteness" the norm, and overcoming racism in the housing market and the economy.

No dialogue with Critical Race Theory happens if it is not with an eye towards what law and theories about the law have to do with the interests of the Black community. I think that I will have succeeded in making the case for how Critical Race Theory embodies many of the core Constitutional and Christian suppositions, that it is only subversive insofar as these venerable institutions are subversive. (Perhaps they all are subversive insofar as they function to undermine the power-grabbing status quo.) But the real dialogue I have in mind with Critical Race Theory will be completed only when readers and the Black community as a whole find the best ways to use these insights in the struggle against racism and to the benefit of the Black community.

It may be that *Newsweek* columnist Marcus Johnson was and still is correct when he claimed in 22021 that the debate over CRT is really about who gets to define what it means to be an American and who gets to define how U.S. institutions work. We need to make sure that the Black voice plays a critical role in these tasks, so that what it means to be American and how its institutions work are not just the result of white input. Let's plunge into that task together, first by coming to terms with what Critical Race Theory really is and teaches, rather than believing everything America says about it.

Chapter 2

Critical Race Theory: What It Teaches and How It Began

We have reviewed what the critics say about Critical Race Theory (CRT). Now let's get to the facts. Critical Race Theory is not the product of a bunch of un-American, unpatriotic Communists out to undermine American jurisprudence and scar children in the educational system! Indeed it is the offspring of the research, interdisciplinary study, and experience of a distinguished group of Civil Rights lawyers and law-school professors. (Of course those drawn to those legal specialties have been known to be a bit liberal.) But in fact, as I've already indicated, a major thrust of this book is to show that a lot of the insights of Critical Race Theory are as American as our Founders, the first slaves arriving in one of the English colonies (Virginia) in 1619, Martin Luther King Jr., fried chicken, and jazz.

Conservatives should be happy with Critical Race Theorists, at least in one way. A major part of their overall agenda, critically to assess the intersection of race and law in the United States, is to criticize liberalism. Indeed, though indebted to the inspiration of W. E. B. DuBois and the heritage of the NAACP along with the Civil Rights Movement, some CRT practitioners, influenced by Black Natioanlist literature of the 1960s and the work of Malcom X and Stokely Carmichael, even at times critique these icons along with the Right.

How did Critical Race Theory get started? We've already pointed to some of CRT's origins in the yearning for freedom that is as old as the African-American community and the Black church, but the movement began to take shape first in the late 1970s and early in 1980 in the work of one of Harvard Law School's first tenured professors Derrick A. Bell, Jr. and a Mexican-American professor at the University of Alabama Law School, Richard Delgado. Both were put off by the fact that advances won by the Civil Rights Movement had stalled, while at the same time, the Black Power Movement was gaining attention. Other early figures in the movement included Alan Freeman of the University of Buffalo, an admirer of Bell's, and Columbia's Kimberlé Williams Crenshaw, as well as Consumer Advocate and Columbia Law School professor Patricia Williams.

In the 1970s, prior to the earliest organization of the movement, there had been a lot of debate in law schools over what racial discrimination is. The legacy of the Civil Rights Movement had led to the definition of it in terms of intentional government (or economic) action to discriminate against others because of their race, ethnicity, gender. But others argued that in making judgments about discrimination, a test should be used as to whether the legislation or policy led to predictable racially skewed results, burdening people of color. This question is very much at the core of Critical Race Theory and the debate about it, not to mention our present controversies over racism. Eminent liberal commentator Victor Ray explains the CRT agenda in another way: He claims it developed in order to understand why the legal victories of the Civil Rights Movement did not always lead to lasting improvements in the lives of people of color (pp. xix-xx).

One turning point in the organization of the movement of adherents formulating Critical Race Theory was a controversy at Harvard, which emerged in 1980 when Bell left the school, and the Harvard administration did not replace him with another African-American legal scholar. Besides attracting Black students at the law school and his eminent career as a Civil Rights lawyer with the NAACP, he had become a controversial figure raising questions about the Civil Rights Movement's legacy, suggesting that the Movement had largely succeeded because integration was in white self-interest (1980). In fact, more recently, one of his intellectual heirs, John Calmore, has warned that integrated settings lead African Americans to inauthenticity. Indeed, what we call integration is really enforced assimilation (Crenshaw et al., pp.321,326).

As we'll see, this point is a core commitment of Critical Race, but not as controversial as most people think it is. Bell's other particularly engaging point was to raise the question of whether integration really had been in the best interests of Black children 1976: 470-516). A 2019 study finding that the Black child is 1.5 to 2 grade levels lower than the average white child compared to Black children lagging behind whites between 1 to 3 years as reported in 1967 by M. L. King (long before integration in the South was still widely implemented) suggests the continuing validity of Derrick Bell's pointed question.

In any case, Black Harvard students disgusted by the fact that they would have no role model to press these questions with after Bell's departure (for greener pastures in law school administration) organized an alternative course taught by successful African-American lawyers. The fact that all this happened on the watch of a Harvard administration and white law-school faculty with liberal political dispositions certainly fed into the growing suspicions about the advisability of Black-white collaboration which the Black Power Movement had already raised in segments of the African-American community influenced by the movement's militancy. Certainly these separatist propensities can be seen as related to the Critical Race Theory at times, though they certainly do not define the movement.

The other development crucial in the origins of Critical Race Theory was the development of the Critical Legal Studies movement, which organized conferences in the 1980s for those in the legal community interested in their agenda. Leaders of the Critical Legal Studies movement rooted their work in earlier American legal scholars' challenges to the sheer objectivity of legal judgments on the grounds that legal decisions are not so much based on law, but on what is deemed a sense of fairness, that the law is ultimately a tool of the economically powerful. These insights aided the movement's leaders in their primary concern "with the relationship of legal scholarship and practice to the struggle to create a more humane, egalitarian, and democratic society." (Kennedy and Klare, 1984: 461). These commitments emerged from their perception that the domination of women by men, or nonwhites, and the poor by the wealthy operate through "apparently neutral language and institutions," masking the relationship of power and control ("Critical Legal Studies Movement"). Major figures in the development of the movement's organizing conferences were the Brazilian-American Harvard Law School professor Roberto M. Unger, Robert W. Gordon, later a Stanford Law School professor, Harvard Law School professor Duncan Kennedy, and Alan Freeman of the State University of New York and formerly at the University of Minnesota.

Although the nucleus of the movement was white, Freeman did write an influential critique of Supreme Court decisions which actually legitimized racism (1978: 804ff.). This article attracted interest from a number of Black legal scholars who would later play a role in the development of Critical Race Theory. As a result, it is not surprising that African Americans did participate in some of the first conferences initiated on Critical Legal Studies.

Scholars who endorsed Critical Legal Studies basically agreed on four principles:

1. Seek to demonstrate the indeterminacy of legal doctrine and show how any given set of legal principles can be used to yield competing or contradictory results.

2. Undertake historical, socioeconomic and psychological analyses to identify how particular groups and institutions benefit from legal decisions despite the indeterminacy of legal doctrines.

3. Expose how legal analysis and legal culture mystify outsiders and work to make legal results seem legitimate.

4. Elucidate new or previously disfavored social visions and argue for their realization in legal and political practices in part by making them part of legal strategy. Related to this principle is the commitment to

> hearing the voice of those who have been discriminated against and
> taking bearing from those voices in legal judgments (in Crenshaw et
> al., p.63).

Not surprisingly there is clearly a critical perspective on the law in these commitments. Laws do not just mean one thing or have just one use. Every law requires constant analysis of its likely results, and so we should ever be suspicious of how a law may be profiting those in power, helping to maintain inequalities of wealth, and then try to do something about the matter (Matsuda, in Crenshaw et al., p.64).

In the background of these commitments, the lawyers were indebted to three twentieth-century European Philosophers whose views of language and government prefigure the critical perspectives of Critical Legal Studies and Critical Race Theory – Jacques Derrida, Michel Foucault, and Antonio Gramsci. Collectively, they are the brain trust for the theory of Postmodernism – a movement aiming to undermine the modern ethos and its commitments to science, reason, individualism, and objective theory (see Swain and Schorr, pp.23-24,99). The Frenchman Derrida is said to be the forefather of the Philosophical School of DeConstruction, a cause célèbre in the American university system and a curse for the Right. Essentially, Derrida (*Grammatology*) insisted that any written text contains several irreconcilable and contradictory meanings. Thus, texts have more than one valid interpretation, and the text links these interpretations together.

These commitments entail for Derrida, as for most scholarship in the Humanities since the time of the German Enlightenment Philosopher Immanuel Kant (1787, pp.257ff.), that the meaning of a text does not reside with the author's intentions because meaning is dependent on the interaction between the reader and the text, and so the meaning of the text and its words is always in flux. Of course, an interpretive reading cannot go beyond a certain point. This indebtedness to Kant by these critical thinkers might be deemed problematic, as he uttered many racist comments early in his career and was a central figure in the development of the theory of racism (see his *Von der verschiednene Rassen der Menschen*, 1775, though taking it back in later years in 1795). (See the links made between Kant and CRT noted recently in 2021 by Marc Thiessen in *The Washington Post.*)

Nevertheless, the DeConstruction method still holds that meaning is subjective or contextual to some extent, and so accepted truths must be called into question. Like all language and texts, we must see how they are used. This entails that we see how these accepted truths (e.g., God, truth, justice, rights, etc.) are culturally conditioned. At the same time, it is important to recognize how they function to exclude some things that the cultural gurus do want to happen. These convictions, including the belief that legal ideology is a reflection of the agenda of a society's elites, have been applied to the legal system by the Neo-Marxist Antonio Gramsci (1971, p.238). He has had a significant impact on Critical Legal Theory (Crenshaw in Crenshaw et al., p.108). The implications of this commitment and Derrida's other views on Critical Legal Theory should already be apparent, and their impact on Critical Race Theory will become evident shortly, when we start looking at its core commitments.

Despite differences with Derrida, Michel Foucault shares many of Derrida's convictions about accepted truths and society's role in formulating them. Thus he rejects a universal basis for a concept of justice. In fact the key concept for him is power. It is in his view a force relation. Power results from inequality. It pervades society and is constituted through accepted forms of knowledge and truth (2011). Foucault teaches us and Critical Legal Theory that power shapes our way of thinking and acting, and by increasing this awareness, we may be better able to change our way of thinking and acting. What seems like justice and common sense is somebody exerting power over us, and the more we know it, the freer we can be.

Italian Communist Philosopher Antonio Gramsci makes his influence felt on Critical Race Theory through his previously noted impact on CRT's forerunner Critical Legal Theory not so much with his Marxism as with his concept of cultural hegemony, which describes how the state and ruling capitalist class (the bourgeoisie) use cultural institutions to maintain power in capitalist societies. The bourgeoisie, in Gramsci's view, develops a hegemonic culture using ideology, rather than violence, economic force, or coercion. Hegemonic culture propagates its own values and norms so that they become the "common sense" values of all and thus maintain the *status quo*. Cultural hegemony is therefore used to maintain consent to the capitalist order, rather than the use of force to maintain order. This cultural hegemony is produced and reproduced by the dominant class through the institutions that form the superstructure (esp. p.238).

A thinker influential on Gramsci and others, Max Horkheimer, claimed in his 1993 article, "Traditional and Critical Theory" that truth is created by the wealthy. From this viewpoint, Gramsci (n.d.) then added that liberation could then be achieved by influencing and transforming society's major capitalist institutions. There are some interpreters who contend that another Marxist indebted to the Frankfurt School of Theology like those just noted, Herbert Marcuse, is an influence on Critical Legal Studies in his claim that violence is built into the very structures of constitutional societies (pp.75-76; AliSafaat and Istiqomah, 2022).

In impacting Critical Legal Studies, the insights of all these philosophers have also shaped Critical Race Theory as we shall see. For Critical Race Theory emerged from the reflections of a group of Black lawyers in the Critical Legal

Studies meetings who had formed a distinct Black interest group. The reasons are familiar to those aware of Black Power suppositions. As a predominantly white-led movement, Critical Legal Studies made Black participants feel marginalized, for too often Black interests were spoken about without really hearing their voices. Black legal scholars wanted to be listened to (see Dalton, 1987: 436-439, in Crenshaw et al., pp.81-82). Even liberal white lawyers, not unlike most white groups, are used to controlling the agenda. The development of Critical Race Studies has been precisely the vehicle to make that happen. Thus it embodies in its origins Black self-autonomy, Black Power in a legal setting aiming to apply these insights to transforming society as a whole. My guess is that its critics got/get nervous whenever the subject of Black Power has been raised. Kimberlé Crenshaw of Columbia Law School is usually identified as the originator of the term Critical Race Theory (Fortin).

From this starting point, the movement began taking off, first with careful analyses of Harvard Law Professor Derrick Bell's and State University of New York legal scholar Alan Freeman's work on how Supreme Court decisions in favor of civil rights were not in Black self-interest. These commitments appeared in the work of Georgetown law professor Charles Lawrence and Kimberlé Crenshaw, and their articles appeared in the 1990s on moving beyond Critical Legal Studies (Cook) and that whiteness is a beneficial social property (Harris). By 1995, not only had workshops for interested lawyers been instituted on the intersection of Critical Theory, racism, and law, but the insights gained were being applied in other fields like education. Some American law schools were beginning to offer Critical Race Theory courses, and Civil Rights advocates internationally were beginning to take note.

The international, interdisciplinary application and development of Critical Race Theory makes special sense in view of the theory's indebtedness to Critical Legal Studies and intellectuals like Jacques Derrida, Herbert Marcuse, and Antonio Gramsci. All of them aimed at changing everything in society through revolutionary practice, integrating their ideas into not just law but also into culture (Horkheimer).

With this background on the development of the movement, we are now ready to review and can better appreciate exactly what Critical Race Theory advocates. At this point, we need to be reminded that even leaders in this movement like Gary Peller (telephone interview, Jan. 26, 2023) highlight that CRT is a spectrum of more critical and less critical perspectives towards American jurisprudence. If white readers can keep in mind this CRT diversity and put aside their sense of entitlement and belief in the fairness of our legal and economic processes, they may be surprised by how, despite or because of its critical rhetoric about the American legal system, CRT reflects Constitutional suppositions and even shares a number of principles with Christian faith. This book is about having you discern these points of contact. But for now let's get clear on what Critical Race Theory really is saying (and you'll begin to recognize how a lot of the stereotypes in pop culture [some you may have brought to the book] will begin to fade).

Core Commitments of The Movement

In their premiere introduction to the movement, two of its members, Richard Delgado and Jean Stefancic, refer to Critical Race Theory (CRT) as "a collection of activists and scholars engaged in studying and transforming the relationship between race, racism, and power." They proceed to note that CRT places these issues in a broader perspective that includes history and economics (p.3). Then Delgado and Stefancic make an important point regarding what is really distinct about the movement, how it differs from traditional Civil Rights endeavors. For while most Civil Rights strategies have sought step-by-step progress within the existing system, CRT "questions the very foundations of the liberal order, including equality theory, legal reasoning, Enlightenment rationalism, and neutral principles of constitutional law." (Delgado and Stefancic, p.3; Lawrence, 1992: 2252ff, in Crenshaw et al, pp.338ff.)

Ah ha, now we've got CRT in its radicalism. It questions objectivity, reason, the foundations of our society, and even Constitutional law. It sure sounds subversive. The critics on the Right are correct.

Of course this sort of rhetoric is not unheard of in the academy these days. It is what observers often call Post-Modernism. The suppositions are clearly indebted to the philosophical influences on CRT we have discussed. Certainly, the DeConstruction Method of Derrida which dominates in many college English Departments and in some Philosophy and Religion Departments endorses the end of objectivity. Meaning is indeed a function of our interaction with reality, and when we see reality that way of course we are led to conclude that "accepted truths" must be challenged. Is this not what critical thinkers are supposed to do, why we send our children to college to get educated?

Applying these insights to legal matters is right in line with the philosophical suppositions of two other previously mentioned influences on CRT, Michel Foucault and Antonio Gramsci. Both of them reject a universal basis of justice, understanding that power shapes our way of thinking, and the state uses its power to maintain the power of those who have it. No, the proponents of Critical Race Theory are certainly not far to the left in the academy. The Right might call them out for relativism, and I'll have some reservations to raise as we proceed. But in view of a 2021 Barna Research poll which found that 54% of Americans believe that truth is subjective, CRT is hardly out of line with mainstream (at least with educated mainstream) America.

For all its roots in Black Pride, Critical Race Theory is not a celebration of differences in biological ethnicity. Indeed, it is argued by most of these scholars that **race is not a biological reality. It is a social construct**, the product of society wanting to segregate certain people to the bottom in order to do the dirty work so that the other segment of the population with light complexions could prosper (Delgado and Stefancic, p.21; also see Calmore, in Crenshaw et al, p.318; Lee, in *Ibid.*, p.442, in connection with an analysis of Kwame Appiah's Ontology of Race).

There is a lot of historical and biological evidence on the side of this conclusion. "Race" is a term for categorizing differences between human beings which was not used in the English language until late in the sixteenth century. Until the 1700s, "race" had a generalized meaning similar to saying that people were of different types. But by then it came to be a terms used for sorting and ranking peoples in the English colonies. Europeans saw themselves as free, while those enslaved belonged to different races not suited for freedom! The completion of the Human Genome Project in 2003 confirmed that humans are 99.9% identical in their DNA entailing that there is no genetic basis for distinguishing people by race.

Of course the origins of racial theory in the eighteenth century in providing political justification for slavery seems to verify CRT's claim that "racial ideology fosters white racial domination" (Gotanda, p.1). Whenever you talk about race or employ its categories on people, you are unwittingly buying into white supremacy. One advocate for Critical Race Theory, Georgetown Law Professor Charles Lawrence (1987, in Crenshaw et al., pp.237-238,240-241), contends that it is the saturation of this cultural heritage by Americans which makes us all racists, at least sub-consciously, and many whites try to repress this reality. A recent book I wrote with Civil Rights leader James Woodall (*Racism in the Mind?)* will help you see how that works itself out in everyday life and what to do about it. But the Critical Race Theory proponents want to warn us, the legal profession, and society at large about the dangers of these categories, though there are voices in the movement like that of the University of North Carolina Law Professor John Calmore seeking to remind us that we do not want us to forget that Black and white are tied to different cultures (Calmore, in Crenshaw et al., p.315).

To be sure, there are debates about whether the total abolition of racial categories is in Black self-interest, for in some contexts race can have a positive binding function as race is socially constructed (Lee, in *Ibid.*, pp.442-443). And it is recognized by CRT proponents that if racial categories were dropped, that will not entail the disappearance of racial inequalities (Ray, pp.4-5). Jayne Lee suggests it may be best to examine how categories of race are being used in assessing and critiquing legal judgment (p.446). But John Calmore (Crenshaw et al., pp.318,320) also wants us to be aware, then, that white experience not be endorsed as universal. This is why he and like-minded colleagues want to be sure that Blacks define themselves, and must not allow those infected by race to do it for them.

Once you have this insight about the role of racial ideology and its impact, then Civil Rights legislation, Liberalism's efforts to strengthen these laws, government characterization of the citizenry on the grounds of race, and even the racial classifications most of us make in everyday life must come under suspicion. Given the origins of racial categories and their continuing use, "White is right (rich, smart, assiduous, and beautiful)" and Black is outside the mainstream, poor, uneducated, unattractive, and lazy, make diabolically logical sense. Throw in Greek philosophy and its dualisms which permeate Western society, prioritizing the rational over the physical, and then Blacks come to be distinguished by the athleticism and ability to entertain, and the domain of whites is said to be the life of the mind.

It is evident that CRT scholars are correct in contending about the **centrality of racism** (Delgado and Stefancic, p.10). In other words, racism is not just about actions and intentions, but rather is embedded in our systems, not just our laws, but also in our cultural cues and subconscious. This view of racism is in line with the analysis of several recent studies by leading scholars of racism like David Maxwell (*Race in Post-Obama America*), Jeannine Hill Fletcher (*The Sin of White Supremacy*), Kelly B. Douglas (*Stand Your Ground*), Ian Henry Lopez (*White By Law*), and the works of Willie Jennings (see especially *After Whiteness*). (The subconscious racism posited by CRT is developed more fully in the book titled *Wired For Racism?* in which James Woodall and I showed that we are biologically programmed for racist feelings and behavior by our brains, unless the brain develops better-coping mechanisms.)

Racial distinctions lead to a culture in which the Negro is always deemed less than fully human (Lawrence, 1987, in Crenshaw et al., pp.236,237). In that sense, there is a **structural determinism of race** in this country. This in turn entails, as we have noted, that **racism is even embedded in our legal system**. The system is therefore ill-equipped to address existing injustices. We can see this in the role precedent plays in making legal decisions. If the precedents you cite are unjust, tinged with racist suppositions, then legal judgments based on this will continue to oppress, despite the intentions of the lawyers and jurists (Delgado and Stefancic, pp.31ff.).

Even more striking and problematic for many is the suggestion by some associated with CRT that the idea of tacit or binding consent to the laws is inauthentic (Kennedy, 1990: 705-757, in Crenshaw et al., p.175). This point might be taken as a challenge to our original Constitutional system which presupposes tacit consent of subsequent generations to decisions of America's Founders (James Madison, 1790, in *Papers*, Vol.16, p.149).

These suppositions were not developed de novo by CRT theorists. A school of thought, calling itself Legal Realism, developed in the heritage of Oliver Wendell Holmes, based on his 1897 article appearing *Harvard Law Review*. The Realists contend that legal rules are to be for the benefit of the larger society. For many proponents, these commitments effectively challenged the concept of legal precedent, since no two cases are exactly the same. Indeed in the view of CRT forerunner Derrick Bell (1992: 364ff, in Crenshaw et al., pp.302), this entails that the function of law should be stressed more than the abstract conceptualization of it. Likewise, CRT supporters like Kimberlé Crenshaw (1988, in Crenshaw et al., p.117) claim that the concept of the law as race-neutral or color blind simply allows class and race disparities to remain in place.

In the same view, University of Pennsylvania Law Professor Dorothy Roberts (1991, in Crenshaw et al, p.398) contends that just using Anti-Discrimination suits and tactics allows social patterns and institutions perpetuating the inferior status of Black to remain in place. Other CRT proponents have noted that when The Supreme Court respects local jurisdictions and zoning restrictions (many of which were motivated by racism) in those cases the law allows segregation to remain in place (Ford, in Crenshaw et al., pp.457ff.). This is why in John Calmore's view, integration renders African Americans inauthentic (see *Ibid.*, pp.320-321). These commitments entail that a **Critique of Liberalism** is also required. For even white liberals on politics and racial issues like me typically endorse Affirmative Action and color-blindness. Referring to Critical Legal Studies which have impacted CRT, University of Arizona law professor Robert Williams (117) notes that the regime of legal realists and so liberalism cannot ultimately transform the oppressive character of our social relations. Indeed there is in Liberal circles a kind of naïve confidence in the value-neutral character of U.S. law (Ansell, pp.344-346). Purported allies with this value-system can't be counted on to work for a radically changed system. Indeed, they'll just be inclined to allow minorities to remain in their present subordinate positions. (Delgado and Stefancic, pp.27-28). It is as Kimberlé Crenshaw once put it:

> Liberals and conservatives seemed to see issues of race and law from within the same structure of analysis – namely, a policy that legal rationality could identify and eradicate the biases of race consciousness in social decision-making (Crenshaw et al, p.xvii).

CRT scholars offer another penetrating analysis of why purported allies cannot really be counted on. They along with the entire American professional classes, have bought into the values of self-interest and individualism, which suppresses the variety immigrants bring to the nation. This desire to embrace each other as part of one nation in turn becomes an impediment to a sense of unity with anyone not sharing our self-interests or sharing our immigrant experience (P. Williams, pp.109f.). And then most whites and liberals in particular subscribe to the belief in a meritocracy (the belief that the brightest and the best always succeed) which does not incline them to believe that the system is too imbalanced, not inclined to favor them, for then their success would not be "merited." The idea of a meritocracy implies that the system is neutral. That is also the problem with Affirmative Action, as it implies that such action is a deviation from an otherwise neutral system. When you really examine the system, though, it is full of injustices which continue to perpetuate white privilege (Crenshaw, Gotadna, et al., in Crenshaw et al., p.xxix).

In its **commitment to social justice** characterizing the Critical Race Theory agenda, proponents of this model do not feel they can really trust the white liberal as an ally in reform, for the white liberal will not be able truly to understand the Black experience, and so not be inclined to seek to change the system radically. There is an awareness among the early advocates of CRT, notably Derrick Bell, that change happens when there are **interest convergences** among different factions (Delgado and Stefancic, pp.20ff.108; Bell, 1980). There is no question that Bell was right about how the Brown v Board of Education decision legally to end segregation served not just Black interests but also white interests too. It was important from a national perspective not to have African Americans disillusioned so much that they might not consider going to war with the new emerging enemy of the 1950s, the USSR. The end of segregation also was in national interest internationally as it played well with people in developing nations, helping America's image in the propaganda war with the Communist Block. Economically, ending segregation was also seen as crucial in opening the South to further industrialization and the development of new markets and labor pools.

Whites will support Black causes, it seems, when they are in white interests. But at least for many proponents of Critical Race Theory, those critical of white liberalism, this reality is seen more as a problem than an opportunity. At the very least we must concede that a radical restructuring of American society to end all discrimination which would include reparations is not in the immediate interests of white Americans. Conclusions like this lead to the image of CRT as advocating a kind of separatism (a tendency which insiders claim has softened since the movement's origins in the 1970s [Delgado and Stefancic, p.30]). Proponents clearly opt for the likelihood of the need for ongoing resistance to white hegemony (Bell, 1992, Crenshaw et al., p.308).

Former Republican Iowa Congressman Greg Ganske, for example, has claimed that the movement worsens race relations. And we've noted in the first chapter how the battle cry of the critics of such a perspective in our public schools reject the idea that all whites are racists as separatist and untenable. Of course, as we have observed and noted again in this chapter, that allegation is true. If you are white like me you are a racist in the sense that we are profiting from a system that favors us, and have not stopped it yet. (This is a point my co-author James Woodall and I make in more detail in the recent book I have noted, *Racism in the Mind?,* and that book will also teach you that Neurobiology even demonstrates that our racism is rooted in our minds too.)

On the other hand, Critical Race Theory is inclusive in the sense of positing **intersectional Theory**. This is the idea that race, sex, national origin, and sexual orientation play out in various ways in similar, though distinct fashion, so that African Americans have some affinities to Hispanics, women of all backgrounds, and the gay/lesbian/bisexual community. They may be natural coalition partners, but certainly don't share precisely identical self-interests (Delgado and Stefancic, pp.58ff.; Crenshaw, 1991, in Crenshaw et al., pp.357-383; Calmore, in *Ibid.*, p.320; Crenshaw, 1991, in *Ibid.*, esp. p.358). Movements for social justice do well to move beyond single-issue analyses, but to look for convergences with other victims of structural discrimination (an observation by Ray, pp.106-107).

I'll have more to say about building coalitions with overlapping self-interests in the next chapter and demonstrate to you that it is the American (Constitutional) way. In that sense Critical Race Theory really is as American as apple pie. It is also in line with a lot of Christian and religious thinking. I hope this book will get its proponents to consider these points and become more explicit about them too, as a lot of the culture wars over CRT could be undermined if they did. And in turn these directions might assist proponents of Critical Race Theory in getting more of what they want. First, though, we need to investigate some other core commitments already in place in the theory which function to assist in achieving its aims.

Strategies of Implementation

Most of the strategies for implementation reflect the philosophical and interpretive suppositions of the three European philosophers previously noted – Derrida, Foucault, and Gramsci. All of them challenge the possibility of objective/descriptive interpretation in favor of subjective interpretation or **Standpoint Epistemology**. (For such commitments, see Lawrence, 1992, in Crenshaw et al., pp.338ff.). These commitments receive a lot of criticism from conservatives and even from some liberals committed to the discerning of fairness and justice in our legal system. But a 2021 Barna Research poll confirmed several previous polls indicating that the majority of Americans (now 54%) think that truth is subjective. Consequently critics of CRT at this point are the minority, and the established legal philosophy of Critical Legal Studies was endorsing such thinking well before the emergence of Critical Race Theory.

If CRT proponents are correct, if the legal system and the society it supports are rigged against Blacks, then objective decisions of the court based on laws' original intent or wording will not be to the benefit of African-American interests. In that case, as Charles Lawrence has argued (1987, in Crenshaw et al., p.237), the intention of the laws cannot and should not be the final criterion of justice. Rather, it seems that that criterion should be how laws are experienced, their outcomes. In that case, it is as his CRT cohort John Calmore asserts (in Crenshaw et al., p.320) that extralegal, contextual factors should play a role in legal cases.

A related point in this connection was nicely made in an article by a proponent of CRT, Western State College of Law professor Neil Gotanda (cf. Ray, pp.34ff.). He laments that the Supreme Court in recent decades has endorsed a Color-Blind Constitutionalism in its decisions. This is the result of the Court's use of formal understandings of race not connected to the realities of race oppression when scrutinizing the Constitutionality of a law, practice, or Court judgments. Another CRT colleague Linda Greene of the University of Wisconsin (in Crenshaw et al., p.292) spoke of a "formalism" in late twentieth-century Supreme Court decisions which were made without attention to the impact of these decisions on victims of discrimination. Earlier Derrick Bell had critiqued reliance on abstract legal principles as harmful to Blacks (1992, in *Ibid.*, p.304)

The plea then by Neil Gotanda and colleagues is that in considering Civil Rights and Affirmative Action cases we should assess the matter not just in terms of immediate results (the racial ratios are more equal), but also in terms of remediation of centuries of Black oppression. No longer, then, is Affirmative Action about giving jobs to the less qualified, a view which just reinforces the system's racism and a sense of Black inferiority (P. Williams, pp.140ff). The issue in testing and scrutinizing laws in our unjust society, rectifying the wrongs, should be not equal opportunity but assessing what helps those at the bottom, with what would best assist African-American neighborhoods. We have been too concerned with equality of opportunity than equality of results. (Delgado and Stefancic, p.29; Peller, 1990, in Crenshaw et al, p.151).

Dorothy Roberts (Crenshaw et al., p.404) makes this point in another compelling way. She notes that the right to privacy is not just the right to be exempt from social conditions, but as the government's duty to protect the individual's personhood and to facilitate processes of choice.

These commitments entail the need for Affirmative Action Programs. Such programs are needed, it is said, in order to delegitimate the way in which whiteness often functions as a kind of property which legitimates capital or favors. Affirmative Action is then required to counter-balance this property (Harris, pp.1710ff., in Crenshaw et al, p.288).

Interestingly enough, for all of CRT's critiques and suspicions of the Constitutional system at least one of its proponents, Charles Lawrence, has noted how James Madison's view of factions which comprise society and need to be controlled (*The Federalist Papers*, No.51) in principle should succeed in protecting minority interests. But Lawrence laments that racist prejudices and the vilification of Blacks prevents groups from forming coalitions with Black interests (1987, in Crenshaw et al., p.242). Another CRT proponent Richard Ford (*Ibid.*, p.450) articulates some openness to Constitutional principles in arguing that the best political thought seeks mediation of conflicts. More on that point in the next chapter.

To some extent, it seems that history could be invoked to support Lawrence's pessimism, and he has plenty of support from other CRT proponents. Linda Greene (*Ibid.*, p.300) observes that the existing legal framework in America "may immorally and unduly dampen the aspiration of African Americans for moral freedom." Derrick Bell even spoke of the need for a Racial Realism (based on Legal Realism we have previously examined) which recognizes that Black people will never gain full equality (1992, *Ibid.*, pp.306,307)! The best which might be achieved, he contended, is temporary peaks and progress. The formalist model of equal rights is not possible in the existing legal framework, he contends. Indeed, commitment to racial equality perpetuates Black disempowerment. We have a system which does not guarantee equal rights. Economic analyses by Richard Ford (*Ibid.*, pp.452-454) demonstrate how a residential segregation no longer founded on Racial suppositions still makes it impossible to overcome segregation due to economic barriers erected between segregated communities. This is the kind of rhetoric that has the Right upset. These lawyers and their followers sound so anti-American, with no respect for our Constitutional and legal system! But there is more that CRT says on this issue and more examination we need to give to the Constitutional system in the next chapter. Maybe the Founders were as realistic as CRT Racial Realism.

One interpreter of Derrick Bell, Dorothy Roberts (1997:1769-1770) understands Bell as siding with Malcom X in viewing that Blacks waste their time appealing to the Constitution, which was never meant to include them. In any case, Bell and CRT as a whole still call for resistance to oppression, urging that the resistance continue even if oppression is never overcome. It so reminds me of comments heard regularly from 1960s Atlanta Student Movement leader and friend Lonnie King, warning any and all that the quest for freedom "is not a sprint. It's a long-distance run," he would say. Suppose lovers of justice undertook with CRT advocates "the long-distance run" of engaging all the different interests of the various factions which make up American society in fresh, creative, interesting ways, always with the aim of making things fairer and more inclusive. The more interesting and intriguing the interests that we could offer American society as a whole, the harder it would be for options seeking oppression to dominate the masses. Another CRT colleague of Roberts, Charles Lawrence (1992, in Crenshaw et al., p.350), has contended that Black radicalism offers a Word which is really the gift to dream.

Is this kind of dreaming not what happened during the Civil Rights Movement, when the marchers offered much more attractive interests and options to the American public than did the Jim Crow advocates? For a brief time in 2020 the Black Lives Matter movement seemed to be offering new alternatives. But alas the American public (and human beings) are fickle with their interests. And approaches with Civil Rights Movement overtones are no longer fresh, perhaps less attractive to the interests of the public today.

Some CRT writers suggest ways to explore in seeking to develop the kind of interests that could build coalitions. John Calmore has noted that Black and white cultures are different (in Crenshaw et al., pp.315). But then he proceeds to suggest that reliance on the Black cultural heritage might aid a social critique (*Ibid.*, p.319). In stressing this point and insisting that Blacks need the power to define themselves and proudly self-identify with their Blackness as Kimberlé Crenshaw advocates (1991, in *Ibid.*, p.375), in functioning as an oppositional movement to racism through Black otherness, CRT could perhaps (maybe it has already when we consider the media and educational stir it has caused) provide the kind of interesting alternatives which might capture the interests of other American interests (see Calmore, in *Ibid.*, pp.320,326). Of course in seeking to build such coalitions of interest convergences we must not forget the observation of Sociologist Victor Ray (pp.68-69) based on Nelson Bell's arguments that minority group rights in America to date have always been revocable, are still subject to the majority's whims.

In executing these strategies of assessing society and law, looking at these realities from the bottom, proponents of Critical Race Theory advocate the use of **storytelling and "naming one's own reality."** (Delgado and Stefancic, pp.44ff.; Charles Lawrence, 1992, in Crenshaw et al, pp.340,343ff.). This model of communication is certainly in line with the narrative, story-telling traditions of Black culture and the Black church. Narratives are said to provide contextualization. When we consider a case for the context of a race-neutral society as American law purports, then data about a dearth of Black wealth or Black businesses is likely to be regarded as a function of lack of Black accomplishment. But when these data are examined in relation to stories of

Black fear or white harassment, pertaining to resources to which many Blacks may have never had access, then the data cited begin to look different (Lawrence, 1992, in *Ibid.*, p.345). Besides, the dominant stories about America which serve white interests need to be counter-balanced (Ray, p.91).

Some have critiqued this proposed means of communication, ostracizing Critical Race Theory for its emphasis on storytelling rather than on testable, measurable data (Farber and Sherry; Lawrence, 1992. in Crenshaw et al, p.346). But experienced trial lawyers will tell you that a big part of arguing cases is to present the facts in the form of a coherent narrative for the jury. And evidence drawn from Neurobiology indicates that stories are the best means of communication, for they put the brains of the storyteller and the hearer in sync (Stephens et al). As we'll see, this commitment to Critical Race Theory also puts it in line with Christian thinking, a convergence that could facilitate the theory's impact and effectiveness in American life if we could get the word out.

The links between CRT and Christian convictions have been first suggested by Georgetown University Law Professor Anthony Cook. In dealing realistically with the implementation of the aims of Critical Race Theory, he sees links between Martin Luther King's work in relation to the Evangelicalism of the Civil Rights era and CRT's agenda in relation to political liberalism. Just as Critical Race Theory needs to deconstruct the fixed agendas of law today and recognize how existing American institutions have oppressed the Black community so that a new alternative must be developed, this was also King's agenda. Another CRT proponent, Kimberlé Crenshaw argues that what we need is to create counter-movements within the dominant ideology which create potential for change (1988, in Crenshaw et al., p.119).

In a more recent article, Crenshaw even went so far as to contend that King himself was a Critical Race Theorist before the concept was formally developed. For she notes that the great Civil Rights leader understood that "the doctrine of white supremacy was embedded in every textbook..." (2022, quoting from King's 1967 book, *Where Do We God from Here?*). He is also cited as observing in the same year that racism "Was not a consequence of superficial prejudice but was systemic." (*Ibid.*, quoting from King's "APA Annual Convention Address) There seems to be clear evidence here for contending that in opting for the structural racism CRT is not breaking with King. We will have more to say about that in a subsequent chapter.

M. L. King's alternative vision to structural racism, rooted in the religious experience of conversion (according to Cook) was the ideal of the "Beloved Community," an ideal which was really a critique of the existing order. Indeed it expanded the best in liberal hopes and dreams for a community of equal rights. King's vision would move beyond such a realm to mutual care and respect for each other, for mere laws cannot change the heart of the oppressor.

Such a model of life together could also enhance self-respect of the oppressed, for no more would they live in the scepter of inferiority or shame. It is this mode which needs to be developed in America as the proponents of Critical Race Theory seek to implement their agenda for overcoming white supremacy. Cook's reflections here seem in line with Lawrence's idea of Black radicalism as providing a dream for freedom fighting.

But with such idealism King was also a pragmatist, again not unlike CRT proponents. He appreciated sin in a way not unlike CRT does in challenging amendments to our present system, recognizing that the socially constructed character of racism is so ensconced in America that we may never fully eradicate the subjugation of the Black community to racism. And so King did not believe that the struggle to actualize his idea in history could ever be fully realized. (In the fourth chapter, we'll see how good solid theology such an insight is.) However, he did believe that the struggle to actualize the ideal could transform society. This realism may also characterize Critical Race Theory in its efforts to attack white privilege in American society. In his article on King, CRT proponent Anthony Cook (Crenshaw et al., pp.96-97) also recognized King's realism and the depths of human sin in the Civil Rights leader's thought.

Western State University College of Law Professor Neal Gotanda (in *Ibid.*, p.257) offered a thoughtful point in connection with exploring CRT strategies for implementing its efforts to end racism in American society. Linking the agenda of Critical Race Theory to how the practice of religion is protected, he suggests how existing precedents could be used to justify anti-racist legislation and strategies. He suggests that just as the Constitution upholds freedom of religion without establishing one religion, so the Supreme Court could allow for a wide range of cultural and ethnic practices but be vigilant that the ways of white supremacy are not established or sanctioned by an openness to variety in the laws and political formulas regarding racial diversity. A fascinating, Constitutionally related proposal. Of course, the critics might question why we need it. Who says American society is inherently racist? This is precisely the concern which underlies all the controversy about Critical Race Theory in our schools. Many whites and Blacks who have "made it" don't want youth exposed to such claims and the kind of disturbing data which follows.

Critical Race Theory Is Right About America's Racism: Here Are the Facts!

The best way to close this chapter is to assess the accuracy of Critical Race Theory's claims about the racist character of American society and its legal system, how it favors whites. No point in trying to defend an agenda which contends that in their present form American laws and norms favor whites, and so require change if the claim can't be verified. Besides, critics are demanding such evidence (Swain and Schorr, pp.13-14).

Of course, we are all well aware of the present inequities of employment, wealth, health care, and incarceration rates. Unemployment rates were higher for Blacks in January 2024– 3.4% for whites and 5.3% for Blacks. This disparity is not about the pandemic, as in 2019 the Black rate was 6.1% and 3.7% for whites. African Americans do not make as much money as their white counterparts. A 2023 U. S. Bureau of Labor Statistics report on median weekly earnings noted that, on average, Black workers earned 76% of what their white counterparts made. If you try to argue that Black Americans are less educated proportionately and so have, on average, less well-paying jobs, that does not work. The most recent study of the matter in a 2022 study of the Economic Policy Institute showed that Black college-educated workers make only 84% of what their white college-educated peers make.

Even superior credentials don't seem to insulate African Americans from these trends. A 2015 study by Michael Gaddis (1451-1479) found that Black Ivy League graduates are only called back for job interviews at a rate that white grads of State flagship universities receive, and that if the Ivy League graduates get the job it is at a lower salary and less prestigious position than whites are characteristically awarded. Sociologists Devah Pager and Lincoln Quillian (355-380) found that white men with a criminal record were more likely to be called back for an entry-level job than a Black without such a criminal record. There is little indication times have changed in nearly 2 decades. The present American legal system seems to permit all these injustices to happen.

All this translates into a Black-white wealth gap. A 2022 study of the Brookings Institute found that the median older white American had $251,000 more wealth than a Black counterpart. A significant reason for this gap relates to the bad start Black families got in slavery and the Jim Crow era segregation, which kept many locked into share-cropping. But that is by no means the whole story, and here is where Critical Race Theory's hypotheses about the law's role in fostering this kind of economic white supremacy seems vindicated. Consider how single-parent families are more likely to be poorer than families in which the parents live together. Our welfare laws financially discourage single mothers with children from marrying, and in cases where the marriage is on the rocks, she might get more government financial aid single than she would with an underemployed spouse.

We need to return to the Roosevelt administration's New Deal for other indications of the racist implications of even widely-popular programs like Social Security and later the GI Bill. It seems then when Social Security was first created, workers in agricultural and housekeeping jobs were not eligible. In the 1930s, these were precisely the jobs which the majority of African Americans held. Consequently, Blacks were effectively excluded from Social Security benefits in its first decades. True, changes have been implemented in the program since the 1960s to include workers in these fields. But it is still the case that Black families have lost a generation or two of wealth accumulation as a result. Consider the extra money spent by these families on the elders from the 1930s through the 1950s, money which might have been used to save or invest. Even if we grant that the original reason for the exclusion of these jobs from Social Security did not have a racist intent, but was a function of difficulties in collecting taxes given the occasional nature of many of these jobs (certainly a debatable point), the outcome of this law is that white privilege was enhanced.

Same scenario regarding Unemployment insurance, which in its New Deal origins also left out workers in the agricultural and housekeeping fields. Again, Black families bear the disproportionate penalty of this oversight, which has also been restored. The latest scholarship on the rationale for the original legislation suggests that it was drafted by unemployment insurers who noted that other nations with such legislation had excluded these occupations. No matter the original intent, though, these laws clearly privileged whites statistically. And the amendments to the programs have not to date (short of reparations) compensated Black families for the wealth lost by their exclusion from these benefits. Proponents of Critical Race Theory are correct, are they not? American laws have created (or at least help maintain) a society of white privilege, a racist society.

The much-loved GI Bill was not much different. Many of the over 1.1 million Black Americans in uniform during World War II were denied benefits – money for education and training and loan guarantees for homes, farms or businesses. But because of political compromises with Southern States, the State governments were given authority to administer benefits, and of course that led to the exclusion of African Americans as beneficiaries in these States. For example, of the 3,229 GI Bill loans for homes or businesses distributed in 1947 in Mississippi, only 2 went to Black veterans (reported in Ray, p.79).

Speaking of inequities in housing, redlining was effectively implemented by the GI Bill and was already in place. It is a decades-long practice of marking maps by race to characterize the risks of lending money and providing insurance in the designated neighborhoods. Thus, mortgages in some areas where African-American vets would apply (esp. predominantly Black neighborhoods) were routinely rejected. As a result, in 1947, only 2 of the more than 3,200 VA-guaranteed home loans in 13 Mississippi cities went to Black borrowers. These impediments were not confined to the South. In New York and the northern New Jersey suburbs, fewer than 100 of the 67,000 mortgages insured by the GI bill supported home purchases by non-whites. This trend continues today, not just with Black vets. As recently as 2021, The Urban Institute reported that 27.1% of Black borrowers who applied were turned down for conventional mortgage loans compared to just 13.6% for all whites. And home ownership is perhaps the most common method of family wealth creation in America.

The dynamics associated with red-lining lead real estate companies and banks systematically to identify property values in Black neighborhoods as of lower value than comparable homes in white ones. The same house in a white neighborhood is appraised at a higher value than if it is located in a predominantly Black neighborhood. And if your house is not as worth as much as the white neighbor's house on the other side of town, you have been cheated of wealth accumulation because of who you are. The system in society as a whole as well as the laws which perpetuate this are rigged against the Black man and woman, right?

Getting loans to start a business is just as difficult as a home loan for African-Americans. Nearly 19% of white business owners started their businesses with a loan from a bank or some other financial institution. But only 15.2% of African-American businesses rely on this sort of financing. Why? Banks don't loan as freely to Black entrepreneurs. Black businesses are twice as likely to be denied loans as white-owned businesses. It seems that up to 95% of Black-owned businesses have been shut out of the government's recent Paycheck Protection Program. There has also been proven discrimination in Department of Agriculture loan policies towards Black farmers. Government policies and the economic dynamics not curtailed by government intervention account for white wealth. The opportunities for African Americans to accumulate it are severely curtailed.

More examples of how the system is rigged: To the question posed by Critical Race Theory about whether Brown v. Board of Education really has helped Black education, the answer seems to be "no." Contrary to a lot of perceptions that the schools are more segregated today than in the 1950s, that is and is not accurate. A far lower percentage of white students attend a school in which whites are 90% or more in the majority. But our kids are more segregated by economics and class. And these dynamics that go along with governmental and institutional policies do work to the detriment of the majority of Black students. Because of the imbalance in wealth and the fact that houses in non-white neighborhoods are not as economically valuable so that the tax base in these neighborhoods is lower. Thus, it follows that the average non-white school district receives $2,226 less per student than a majority-white district, which entails that government educational policies are to the disadvantage of African-American students. Our tax structure and how the funds are dispersed are all about white privilege. And as my co-author James Woodall and I point out in our recent book (*Racism in the Mind?*) our educational system is geared to the ethos of and culture of the educated middle and upper classes and effectively makes their poor and undereducated parents feel uncomfortable and out of place.

All of these factors have implications for health. There are data that suggest that if you are more financially secure, you are likely to live longer. Thus, since there is a Black-white wealth gap, it is not surprising that life expectancy for whites exceeds that of Black by more than 3 years. Another issue in these dynamics relates to the fact that African Americans are less likely to have health insurance. And a Harvard Economist Albert Alesina has argued that a reason we don't have economic and medical safety nets in America like in Western Europe has been because of the perception that Blacks would benefit.

It is well known that in the recent pandemic, African Americans were more likely stricken by the virus. It's been more than twice as likely that you'll die from the virus if you're Black. In part, this may be a function of the fact that, on the whole, African Americans are more plagued by diseases like diabetes, which makes them more vulnerable to COVID than the average white American. But another factor is that while 29.9% of whites held jobs which allowed them to work from home during the pandemic, only 19.7% of African Americans were employed in such positions. Poverty, which disproportionately impacts the Black community, is also bad for your health, as it can lessen the antibodies we have to fight disease and also hasten aging by the waning of our tissue repair mechanisms.

Negative social images attributed to Black people are also bad for their health. It entails that they receive fewer medical procedures, even less pain medication than whites (Hoffman et al., 4296-4300).

Another factor in shorter Black life expectancy relates to the criminal justice system and the likelihood that if you're Black, you're more likely to be shot. You are 2½ times more likely to be shot by police than if you are white. And as of 2022, you are 10 times more likely to be shot in a homicide if you are Black. Another troubling statistic: Police solve homicides of white victims more readily than they do homicides of Black victims. In 63% of white deaths, arrests are made, but only 47% of Black victims had their murderer arrested. Just a coincidence? The system exacerbates these trends. When police shoot a citizen, they effectively first receive a vacation (are placed on administrative leave). This policy is not likely to foster the message that Black Lives Matter.

Present policing policies also make it more likely that Blacks will be under suspicion for crimes and more readily arrested than whites. Certainly the image of the Black man in the media fosters these suspicions, and this has been demonstrated in a study reported in Queu, the journal of the Association of Computing Machinery, which found that ads implying a person had been arrested were more likely to appear in searches for names associated with being Black (see Linn, p.146). Linn (pp.149ff.) provides numerous other examples of how searches for "Black girls" or "Black boys" on the internet (Google, Alexa, etc.) yielded images related to sexual behavior or criminality. We've also already noted how it seems that whites talk about race in private tends towards a considerably more negative assessment of Blacks than typical of white public discourse (Ray, pp. xii-xiii). To this point, Sociologist Eduardo Bonilla-Silva has noted that most whites do not want to be associated with racism, but few want to give up the benefits which came from racialized opportunity-hoarding.

There is another, no less significant reason why present policing policies entail that African Americans are more likely to be under suspicion for crimes. A policy of Comp Stats (statistical policing) used by many police departments, which uses crime statistics to deploy police in the parts of town statically most likely to have crimes, leads to the practice of placing most cops in high crime areas, which tend to be predominantly Black, and so more Black men and women are seen as suspects, more likely to be under surveillance. As a result, it is also no surprise logically that 37% of the prison population in America is Black, though African Americans only comprise 13% of the US population. Then add to that how imprisonment rates for Blacks are much higher than that for whites for the same crime, that nearly half the population on Death Row is Black despite comprising only 12% of the American population.

It's not as simple as pointing to biased judges who have been brain-washed by media images of Blacks as criminals. (Once again, we observe how racism in the media breeds or encourages racial behavior.) The laws are biased in racist ways, as drugs of choice by Blacks have stiffer sentencing guidelines than the drugs whites tend to favor. Is not CRT right? The laws of America seem to foster racism, or at least privilege whites. A similar case can be made regarding the latest Republican efforts to gerrymander Congressional and State House districts to the detriment of the Black vote. In view of the watering-down of the Voting Rights Law and the propensity of the Supreme Court's present majority to interpret the Fourteenth Amendment in a color-blind way (such color-blindness being the unfortunate heritage of the Civil Rights Movement according to leaders of CRT), its recent decision to allow Alabama's redistricting plan to suppress the Black vote in the State comes as no surprise. Critical Race Theory's proponents have another example of how the color-blindness of our present system just supportsexisting white privilege. The system as a whole is supportive of racism.

Next Steps

Should we be concerned that America's youth in our schools learn about the biases of the social and political systems, the way in which white kids profit from it? Is it wrong to teach that self-interest guides people and groups? Are we scarring them to learn about how this has cashed out in history, to teach our children to begin to consider the possibility that a way out of our present problems might be to favor people at the bottom? Actually, as we'll see when we teach them these points, we are actually helping them better learn the U.S. Constitution and even setting the stage for more appreciation of religious commitments on the American scene. Don't worry, though, the chapters ahead will offer some critiques of Critical Race Theory, how the Constitution and the Christian religion, can get us out of the subjectivity of all the philosophers who've influenced CRT and get us looking together for universal truth. Next, let's examine the U.S. Constitution and get it in dialogue with CRT. Though proponents of Critical Race Theory have not made this case (to the detriment of the endorsement of their thinking by the broader public), we'll see that much of what we have been saying about CRT is in line with Constitutional thinking.

Chapter 3

Critical Race Theory and Our Constitutional System: Friends or Enemies?

We have noted in the previous chapter that many proponents of Critical Race Theory strongly critique the racism of our present Constitutional system. We have also observed how critics have taken these observations as "proof" of the anti-American character of CRT. Before adjudicating that debate, we need to examine in detail what the Constitution actually says about slavery and race, and whether its core suppositions are in fact at odds with the agenda/s/ of Critical Race Theory.

Many of us are aware of statements in the Constitution about slavery, and for the Black community and its friends what we find is not pretty. Let's start there, and then try to understand the background of these assertions, to determine whether they forever mar the Constitution as a resource for freedom and equality for the Black community.

Probably the most (in)famous of the original Constitutional clauses pertaining to the Black community emerges in Art. I, Sec.2 – the 3/5s clause. It stipulates that in determining the population of States determining representation in Congress, the number of free persons should be counted along with Indians not paying taxes and 3/5 the number of those in the State "bound to Service for a Term of Years." This has been taken as implying that African Americans are only equal to 3/5 of the value of whites, according to the Constitution.

Also in Article I, in Section 8, we find another reference that had historically been associated with slavery and perhaps its support by the Founders. This is the clause which allows Congress to establish a militia for the purposes of "to execute the Laws of the Union, suppress Insurrections and repel Invasions." This has been taken by critics as the Founders' efforts to repress slave revolts, and so indicates that the founding document was written to protect pro-slavery interests.

Of course, it must be noted that Art. I Sec. 9 did commit to ending the slave trade by 1808 -- 20 years after its ratification. But our nation, supposedly committed to "establishing justice" (Constitution, Preface), did sanction the importation of thousands of additional slaves for its first 20 years and did not abolish slavery. But perhaps the most egregious assertion of the original Constitution is found in Art IV Sec. 2. It states that

> No Person held in Service or Labour in one State under the Laws thereof, escaping into another, shall in Consequence of any Law or regulation therein be discharged from such Service or Labour, but shall be delivered up on Claim of the Party to whom such Service or Labour may be due.

This is the basis of the infamous Fugitive Slave Laws. It certainly seems at first glance that the Founders were intent on preserving slavery. (It might also be added that even the Abolitionist Thirteenth Amendment allows slavery to continue as a punishment for crime.)

All of these passages have been bones of contention in the Black community for centuries, dating back to William Lloyd Garrison's critique of the Constitution. One can see this in Frederick Douglass' 1860 famed speech in Scotland defending the Constitution, as he felt compelled to address each of these texts. We will subsequently review his arguments concerning each of these clauses. But at this point, let's first examine the core suppositions of the Founders at the Constitutional Convention and of James Madison (given his role as Secretary in putting the document together). We will observe a lot of points of contact between these suppositions and those of Critical Race Theory.

Constitutional Common Sense

Historians and students of American government largely agree on the impact of John Locke our founding documents – esp. on The Declaration of Independence. We have documentation of this point from the following resolution from Jefferson's own University, the University of Virginia Board of Visitors (in 1984, p.479), on which he and James Madison were members:

> Resolved, that it is the opinion of the Board that as to the general principles of liberty and the rights of man, in nature and in society, the doctrines of Locke, in his "Essay concerning the true original extent and end of civil government,"...may be considered as those generally approved by our fellow citizens of this, and the United States...

A number of influential pamphlets of the Revolution had already appealed to Locke on natural rights (Otis, 9,12,22-23,26,27,30,37; Hamilton, 1755).

It is clear that from Locke the Founders appropriated the idea that government was obligated to follow the will of the majority (1690, Ch. VIII, 97). Like them, Locke also believed that every citizen was equal in the view of government (Ch. VIII, 95; cf. Ch. II,5). In fact, he went so far as to reject slavery (Ch. IV).

We see Locke's influence in the Continental Congress' Declaration of Independence not only in his advocacy of rebellion when government fails to fulfill its duties (Ch. IXI), but also in the Declaration's famed statement that all men have rights to "life, liberty, and the pursuit of happiness." This was just a slight alteration by Jefferson of Locke's claim that all men have the right to pursue "Life, Liberty, and the Pursuit of Property" (Ch. VII, 87). There is an optimism in Locke's view of human nature, and he even rejects original sin and the idea that we sin in all we do (1731, 4). We are naturally predisposed to care for each other, he asserts (1690, Ch. II, 6). He posits an optimism about how well humans treated each other in the state of nature (Ch. II).

Obviously, this sort of optimism characterizes a lot of the thinking of the Founders. In a 1783 Circular Letter, George Washington well illustrates these commitments. He wrote:

> The citizens of America... are, from this period, to be considered as the actors on a most conspicuous theatre, which seems to be peculiarly designated by providence for the display of greatness and fidelity... The foundation of our empire was not laid in the gloomy age of ignorance and superstition, but at an epoch when the rights of mankind were better understood and more clearly defined than at any former period... At this auspicious period the United States came into existence as a nation, and if their citizens should not be completely free and happy, the fault will be entirely their own.

In *The Federalist Papers* (No.3) John Jay echoed such Enlightenment optimism as he referred to Americans as "intelligent and well-informed" and that such people are unlikely to hold erroneous opinions about their own self-interest for a long period of time.

Not just in the Declaration, but in a 1799 letter (To Will Green Munford) Thomas Jefferson went to the extreme of believing the possibility of the unchecked progress of human beings. He wrote:

> I consider man as formed for society, and endowed by nature with those dispositions which fit him for society. I believe also with Condorcet, as mentioned in your letter, that his mind is perfectible to a degree of which we cannot as yet form any conception.
>
> I join you therefore in branding as cowardly the idea that the human mind is incapable of further advances...

For as long as we may think as we will speak as we think, the condition
of man will proceed in improvement.

The Founders clearly believed that their own generation was virtuous
(Jefferson, 1782, in 1984, p.246; Jefferson, 1814).

Often in pop culture this is the version of the American system embraced and
taught, except among Critical Race Theory and other proponents of critical
thinking who remind us how many of these "virtuous" Founders either owned
slaves or at least sanctioned slavery. There is another strand of the Founders'
thinking – the more realistic strand embedded in The Constitution, influenced
by Madison, John Witherspoon, Puritanism, and the philosophy of Scottish
Common Sense Realism.

Scottish Common Sense Realism

Though Locke's influence on the Founders is indisputable, it is worth noting
that there seems to be no evidence that his books figured in the sent curriculum
of any American college prior to the Revolution (Dunn). And though in his 1740
Proposals Relating to the Education of Youth in Pennsylvania (in n.d., pp.323-
324), Benjamin Franklin recommended a text by Locke in education, he also
recommended texts by the Scottish philosopher Francis Hutcheson pertaining
to ethics and government. Locke was obviously not much of an influence on
Franklin's view of government.

Hutcheson was the mentor to a number of eighteenth-century Scottish
thinkers who started the Enlightenment in their mother land. He had a
significant impact on the founder of a school of Philosophy designated **Scottish
Common Sense Realism**, Thomas Reid (1710-1796). Though Reid seems to
have had just minimal impact on the American scene, several of his students
functioned as popularizers like Dugald Steward and especially John
Witherspoon (the only clergyman to sign The Declaration of independence and
a mentor of Madison) (1774, pp.73-74,97).

This Scottish philosophy actually represented in its origins a reaction against
the skepticism of David Hume and the Idealism of Irish thinker George
Berkeley – the first denying that we can know reality with certainty as all
knowledge is just an inference (IV.1) and the other in a similar way contending
that ordinary objects are only collections of ideas, having reality because they
exist in the human mind and so in the mind of God (6-8,56,57,72). At the same
time, in Germany, Immanuel Kant had been attempting to find a way to critique
these alternatives (1764). As we noted in the previous chapter (see p.14), he
sought a way to find truth and still posit a constructive role for the interpreter
in determining the truth and meaning of what is observed/interpreted.
Common Sense Realism sought an alternative to Kant. And insofar as the

primary philosophical influences on Critical Race Theory through Critical Legal Theory are in line with Kant, it follows that this Common Sense approach is at odds to some extent with CRT.

Common Sense Realism is so named for its commitment to asserting in contrast to these options that the reality of objects we perceive is real and true. It aims to be not the common sense the elites try to impose on us, but the common sense that is dictated by the concrete realities which confront. Its proponents contend that it is common sense to endorse the reality of what we encounter and to trust our perceptions. As Thomas Reid himself once put it (1785,258): "In perception we not only have a notion more or less distinct of the object perceived, but also an irresistible conviction and belief of its existence."

The most vivid perceptions are common sense. And also morality is common sense as well. All human beings are equal in the sense of being able to discern the good. This affirmation was made by both Witherspoon and Reid his mentor, the former referring to the moral sense as "really a principle of nature" (1774; cf. Reid, 1786, pp.580,582,589,595,662,679).

Comments about the "self-evident truths" of The Declaration of Independence may in fact be a function of Jefferson's dialogue with this Scottish philosophy. The phrase in The Declaration is certainly in line with Scottish Common Sense thinking more so than Locke's view of the natural law. And it seems that Scottish moral philosophy was an integral part of the curricula of most American colleges, and this apparently pertains to Virginia. At the College of William and Mary, William Small of Aberdeen taught moral philosophy, and it was primarily under Small that Jefferson did his undergraduate work. "Jefferson spent two of the most influential years of his life studying that entire common-sense system of things' under Small's guidance (Malone, esp. p.55). During that period, Jefferson became acquainted with the works of Common Sense Realist philosopher Francis Hutcheson. Historian Gary Wills (p.201) informs us that Small taught Hutcheson's own discipline by the Scottish Realist's own method and that Hutcheson's works "were regularly in Jefferson's hand."

Nor was Hutcheson the only Scottish writer whose works were familiar to Jefferson. Wills (p.175) makes much of the fact that the basic library list that Jefferson prepared for a friend in 1771—" in just the period when he was replacing his own lost library"—contained works by Thomas Reid, along with books by Adam Smith and David Hume.

Perhaps the clearest manifestation of the influence of Common Sense Realism on our Constitutional system emerges when we consider the origins of this school of Philosophy in the Scottish Presbyterian Church. Although Scotland had become a Presbyterian Kingdom, by the time of the eighteenth century, the church and the kingdom had been embroiled in controversy as a result of the official unification of the Kingdoms of Scotland and England in 1707. This led to the Patronage Act of 1712, which gave powers of appointment to churches in Scotland to the British crown. Obviously, this led to a lot of resistance in Presbyterian churches in Scotland, culminating in the formation of an "Evangelical" or "Populist" segment of the Presbyterian Church, determined to hold on to unique (Orthodox) Presbyterian convictions. The other party termed "Moderates" embraced the government and its new clerical appointment system.

This Moderate group became the ecclesiastical home of the intelligentsia who launched the Scottish Enlightenment, including the leaders of Scottish Common Sense Realist Philosophy. (The fact that Thomas Reid accepted his first pastoral charge as a result of a Royal clerical appointment indicates that he belonged to this group.) If you saw yourself as a Moderate you were by definition open to change, and so no wonder that new ideas breaking with the old Orthodox schools of theology and philosophy emerged from this coalition. But on the other hand, you did not want to be perceived by Evangelical critics and the Scottish populace as a whole as having abandoned the faith. Consequently, Moderates like Reid and his philosophical cohorts maintained at least a nominal orthodox Presbyterian point of view, and these commitments related to sin and human nature seem reflected in their views on government.

This traditional Presbyterian orientation rooted in Calvin includes belief in a sovereign God and the total depravity of human nature (1.4.5; 1.16.1ff.; 2.1.11). He (2.1.8) and his tradition speak of human beings concupiscent, marked by selfish desire in all we do. These themes were picked up by Thomas Reid and the Scottish Common Sense Realists. He embraced a Presbyterian view of Providence, claiming that humans can do nothing that God "does not see fit to permit." (1786, p.616) And elsewhere, when affirming free will, he does so while contending that it must be affirmed in paradox with Predestination (n.d., 977).

Regarding human nature, it is true that at points Reid posited an optimistic view, as he claimed that most people continue to just what nature and their education made them to be (1775). Desires and appetites (such as the desire for power and lust) are said to be in principle morally irrelevant. It is impossible to eradicate them, for they are part of the way God created humans (1786, pp.533-535). But at many other points Reid clearly denies that morality is "simple" in this sense, reducible to ultimate intention. And in those instances, he embraces something like a Presbyterian view as he claimed that selfishness mars outwardly more actions and that to serve God and be useful to humanity, without any concern about our own good, is "beyond the pitch of human nature." (1786, p.585).

We will talk more about how such thinking relates to the historic Western Christian view of Original Sin. At this point, it suffices to note how Reid understands the political implications of this view of human nature. He wrote:

> To conclude, Since we neither live, nor does it seem to be the design of Providence that we shall ever live, in a Utopian Society, but among Men surrounded with Temptations, and whose Interests interfere & cross on another in innumerable Instances, let us not expect Perfection in Individuals, in Societies, or in Government. (1751ff., p.298)

This viewpoint is most in line with Reid's predecessor, Francis Hutcheson, who while positing a common moral sense in all human beings, proceeded to argue that this moral sense is driven by what will promote our own ends, giving us maximum pleasure (1742, pp.32-34,183,236-237). In the American setting, John Witherspoon never spoke of total depravity. But he did claim that all humanity is by nature under sin (in a sermon of that title), contending that "the deplorable wickedness in which the word in general is overwhelmed in a continued stream the first sin of Adam…"

Let's talk further about the vision of politics and government which ensue from these common-sense insights, first by providing more detail on Reid's comments and then back to Witherspoon's thinking. What they have to say is definitely in line with the vision of government we find in the American Constitution.

Reid's realism about human nature led him to think of politics as a rule-governed system. For him, "A Government of Laws [is] better than independence." (1751ff., p.176). Of course this is a function of his realization that a utopian society can never be achieved. This line of thinking is certainly in line with CRT's Racial Realism, and, as we'll see, with the Constitution.

Echoing his mentor Hutcheson (1725, 295), in his view there are certain "inalienable rights" pertinent to liberty, grounded in the law of nature that must be defended by government (1751ff., p.201). One natural right he identifies is equality, and so he rejected slavery (pp.147,223). That a major influence on the US Constitution would be anti-slavery, supporting movements of Abolition, should also be noted in terms of our examination of CRT interpretations of biases in the American system.

On American territory, Common Sense Realist Witherspoon, a direct influence on the Constitution through his student James Madison as we'll note, also articulated in writing his opposition to slavery, calling it "unlawful to make inroads upon others, unprovoked, and take away their liberty by no better right than superior power." (1774, p.125). Yet at the time he made this statement, Witherspoon himself owned property in slaves. He seems to have made a distinction between the act of enslaving people and holding them as property after they had already been enslaved. We need to examine whether this hypocritical commitment to white supremacy has seeped into the Constitutional system, or if Reid's apparently sincere condemnation of slavery is embodied in Constitutional dynamics indebted to the Scottish Common Sense tradition.

Among additional consequences for government entailed by other Common Sense Realist commitments include Reid's openness to emerging democratic trends during his lifetime. In his view, political and moral principles are established by the universal consent of humanity (1786, p.589; 1785, p.589; Stewart, p..384). About this matter Reid wrote:

> Thirdly, I conceive that the consent of the ages and nations of the learned and unlearned, ought to have a great authority with regard to first principles, where every man is a competent judge... When we find general agreement among men, in principles that concern human life, this must have a great authority with every sober mind that loves truth (1785, p.439)

These commitments led Reid to claim that if you have a government that functions efficiently and legally, it does so only because a kind of contract between the people and the rulers has been assumed. There is, then, a kind of "tacit consent" among the governed. Reid wrote:

> A Political Society cannot be justly constituted but by consent express or tacit. How far it is binding upon the posterity of those who first consented to it. A Government unjustly imposed may afterwards acquire Right by "tacit consent." (1751ff., p.177)

We will observe how this theme is embodied in our Constitutional system.

Given these convictions, it is not surprising that Reid contended that kingly government in small territories that degenerate into tyrannies would likely, in his view, change into democracies (Ibid., p.175). He seems to have been a supporter of the French Revolution, at least in a moderately appreciative way. His cautious support of democracy and the French freedom-fighters led him to assume restrained support of political revolution, contending that changes in government should be undertaken only for the most weighty reasons. He wrote:

> If we pull down the old Government... such Changes ought not to be rashly made, but with good Advice & for weighty Causes. (*Ibid.*, p.280)

These suspicions of what human beings do when left totally to their own devices led Reid to opt for a limited democracy. On that matter he wrote:

> Here perhaps it will be said, What has authority to do in matters of opinion? Is truth to be determined by most votes?... I am aware that, in this age, an advocate for authority has a very unfavourable plea; but I wish to give no more authority than its due. Most justly do we honour the names of those benefactors to mankind who have contributed more or less to break the yoke of that authority which deprives men of the natural, the unalienable right to judging for themselves; but, while we indulge a just animosity against this authority, and against all who would subject us to tyranny, let us remember how common the folly is, of going from one faulty extreme into the opposite. (1735, pp.439-440)

Likewise, Reid's Scottish immigrant protégé John Witherspoon made a similar comment, contending that "Pure democracy cannot subsist long nor be carried far into the departments of state – it is very subject to caprice and madness of popular rage." (1815, Vol.7, p.101) Of course, contrary to popular culture American folklore and strands of thinking emanating from The Declaration of Independence, America is not a democracy. Founder John Adams made that clear when he issued the warning that "Remember, democracy never lasts long. It soon wastes, exhausts, and murders itself. There never was a democracy yet that did not commit suicide." (1850-1856, Vol.6, p.484)

Both Reid and Witherspoon posited a kind of constitutional democratic system, even a representational democracy. Each posited something like three branches of government (Reid, 1751ff., pp.295-297; cf. Witherspoon, 1802, Vol.7, p.435). And in accord with Constitutional thinking also posited something like the separation of powers. First, we consider how Witherspoon posited the King's subordination to Constitutional principles:

> The Right of Sovereigns to Respect & to Obedience in things that are lawfull and are not contrary to the Publick Good or to the Constitution. They are not to (be) obeyed in things unlawful... The deeds of the Monarch contrary to the constitution are void and null. (*Ibid.*, pp.251-252)

Witherspoon's words, likely written in 1772 prior to the formulation of the Constitution will certainly ring even truer in American ears. For there can be little doubt that they profoundly impacted his student James Madison, and given Madison's significant impact on the Constitution in his role as the convention's secretary it is hardly surprising that Witherspoon's views reflect in The Constitution. Witherspoon wrote:

Every good form of government must be complex... so that one Principle may check the other... It is folly to expect that a state should be upheld by integrity of all who have a share in managing it. They must be so balanced that when one draws his own interest or inclination, there may be an over poise upon the whole. (1774, p.144)

The Common Sense Realist Philosophers on both sides of the Atlantic, with their cautiousness about the problems associated with a pure democracy, recognized that government functions best when rules are observed which permit a real dialogue and debate among the various segments so that not just some segment's interests can overcome the good of the whole.

Common Sense About Property

Because of this Scottish philosophy's influence on America's Founders and the system they created, several other commitments of Scottish Common Sense Realism are relevant to our examination of the Constitution. Reid and later the American political system lack property qualifications for citizenship. The ideal government in Reid's view would totally reject private ownership. Ever the realist in his assessment of government and the human condition, Reid did recognize the right of private property (1751ff., pp.283-284). He also acknowledged that in such a system property will always be unequally divided. In his view, all evils stem from the pursuit of property. Ultimately, human society is nothing else but "a Scramble for Money." (*Ibid.*, pp.286,295-296)

Given his critical view of property, it is hardly surprising that Reid was no champion of unbridled laissez-faire economics. He endorsed private ownership of property, but insisted that the end of property must be the common good. Property rights must always be measured by this standard (*Ibid.*, pp.251.208,206; Francis Hutcheson, 1725/1971, pp.283f.) However, this endorsement is accompanied by an insistence on government intervention to protect the poor. Reid writes:

[T]he general principle that bargains ought to be left to the judgment of the parties, may admit of some exceptions, when the buyers are the many, the poor, and the simple – the sellers few, rich, and cunning; the former may need the aid of the magistrate to prevent their being oppressed by the latter. (1788)

To the degree Reid's insights reflect in the American Constitutional system, we would have to conclude that it is not as hostile to Black interests as some CRT proponents suggest. Let's see.

The Constitution's Realism

The themes we have been identifying are clearly embedded in the US Constitution. The case for the document's and system it created's common-sense realism seems obvious. But we now need to document this claim with careful attention to the Founders' actual endorsement of Common Sense Realistic claims along with the idealism inherited from Locke and other Enlightenment strands.

We have already noted that not just Locke, but Common Sense Realism impacted Jefferson and other segments of the eighteenth–century Colonial ethos in America through its impact on the curriculum of several early American colleges. In fact, Jefferson once stated in an 1824 letter to Dugald Stewart that the Scottish scholar's book has "become the textbook of most of our [American] colleges & academies." 1984, p.1488) But nowhere else is it more significant for our story than to note what transpired at the College of New Jersey (today's Princeton University). When John Witherspoon became its President, he supplanted Berkeley's books in the curriculum with Reid (for details see Butterfield). James Madison became one of Witherspoon's students, the man who would function as the Secretary of the Constitutional Convention, whose mark on our Constitutional system in this way is undeniable. And it seems that the impact of Witherspoon on his thinking was a deep one (convergences between Scottish Common Sense Realism and the Constitution make that apparent), as in 1769 in a letter to his father Madison claimed that Witherspoon is one who should come to teach all Virginians.

Clearly, a good place to start in documenting Constitutional compatibility with Common Sense Realism is with their shared view of human nature. As we will see further in the next chapter, the Augustinian and Reformation view of sin clearly reflects in both strands.

Pessimism/Realism about human nature is all over the Founders' reflections. In the Debates at the Constitutional Convention (pp.34,52,131,233-234,311-312,322-323), Gouverneur Morris warned against the rich seeking to establish dominion over everyone else, Alexander Hamilton claimed that "men love power," and Benjamin Franklin reminded Convention delegates that men are driven by "ambition and avarice." And in the "Busy-Body No. 4" he wrote that "Almost every Man has a strong Desire of being valu'd and esteem'd by the rest of the Species."

In at least two of his contributions to *The Federalist Papers* (Nos.10,51) (articles aiming to argue the virtues of the Constitution) James Madison applied insights like the ones just noted by other Founders to groups (factions) that emerge in any free society. We see this in his definition of a faction near the beginning of No.10:

By a faction I understand a number of citizens whether amounting to a majority or a minority of the whole who are united and actuated by some common impulse of passion, or interest, adverse to the rights of other citizens, or to the permanent and aggregate interests of the community.

The connection between our fallible reason and self-love makes factions inevitable. To this point, Madison added:

The diversity in the faculties of men, from which the rights of property originate, is not less an insuperable obstacle to a uniformity of interests.

Factions are inevitable in a free government, Madison notes. Freedom is to faction what air is to fire. And he rejects any government that would preclude such freedom.

Of course the Founders did not just draw upon Scottish Common Sense Realism and Christian faith for these insights about human nature. Two other Enlightenment influences having an impact on their thought, David Hume and Lord Montesquieu (Charles-Louis de Secondat) held these realistic views about the selfish character of human beings.

In making these points, Madison joined by other delegates to the Constitutional Convention added that in any society, the factions which develop need to be controlled. This is why in accord with Reid's warnings, they did not espouse a pure democracy (Madison, *The Federalist Papers, No.10)*. On this matter, Madison also wrote *The Federalist Papers*:

Different interests necessarily exist in different classes of citizens. If a majority be united by a common interest, the rights of the minority will be insecure. (No.51)

... there are particular moments in public affairs when the people, stimulated by some irregular passion, or some illicit advantage, or misled by the artful representations of interested men, may call for measures which then themselves will afterwards be the most ready to lament and condemn. (No.63)

Alexander Hamilton (in *The Federalist Papers*, No.71) made a similar point in contending that the majority was prone to give "unqualified complaisance to every sudden breeze of passion, or to every transient impulse which the people may receive from the arts of men, who flatter prejudices to betray their interests."

A pure democracy will lead to the majority faction repressing the rights of minorities. Consequently, the government the Founders aimed to give us would protect these rights. It seems that at least in its intentions, our Constitutional system intends to give CRT proponents precisely what they want. And insofar as all of us are prone to be part of factions which are self-interested, the claim by CRT proponents that Blacks must always be wary of white self-interests in forming any coalition with white citizens seems right in line with the American Constitution. (Whites need to get over their claims to White Innocence when confronted with CRT critiques.)

Of course "the proof is in the pudding," and we need to examine in this light the adequacy for achieving racial justice of the Founders' solution – checks and balances and the separation of power through the different branches of government. After all we have noted that CRT law professor Charles Lawrence (see p.24, above) concedes that James Madison's view of factions that comprise society and need to be controlled (*The Federalist Papers*, No.51) in principle should succeed in protecting minority interests. But due to racial prejudice, the playing field is not fair in Lawrence's view, and so the Black faction is disadvantaged in creating majorities with other factions to create a majority beneficial to Black Americans.

It is clear that Madison was sympathetic to how easy it is to trample on minority rights. For as he noted at point in *The Federalist Papers*, we tend to be emboldened in our view of things when there are a lot of people on our side. We tend not to identify with minority causes. We need government to protect us from the tyranny of the mob:

> If it be true that all governments rest on opinion, it is no less true that the strength of opinion in each individual, and its practical influence on his conduct, depend much on the number which he supposes to have entertained the same opinion. The reason of man, like man himself, is timid and cautious when left alone, and acquires firmness and confidence in proportion to the number with which it is associated. (No.49)

It is evident, then, that we need a government that protects us from ourselves. Madison makes this point in No.#51. He wrote:

> It may be a reflection of on human nature that such devices should be necessary to control the abuses of government. But what is government itself but greatest of all reflections on human nature? If men were angels no government no government would be necessary... In framing a government which is to be administered by men over men, the great

difficulty lies in this: you must enable the government to control the governed; and in the next place oblige it to control itself.

Elsewhere in that treatise, he wrote

Justice is the end of government, It is the end of civil society... In the extended republic of the United States, and among the great variety of interests, parties, and sects which it embraces, a coalition of the majority of the whole society could seldom take place on any other principles than those of justice and the general good, whilst there being less danger to a minor from the will of the major party, there must be less pretext, also, to provide for the security of the former, by introducing into the government a will not dependent on the latter, or, in other words, a will independent of the society itself.

And in Nos.10 and 51 he noted that the greater the number of citizens, voters, and representatives in a republic like the United States, then factious combinations are less to be dreaded as it would be more difficult for them to form.

In short, Madison's and his colleagues' intentions were not to remove factions just to control them. This is certainly in line with Critical Race Theory's thinking that we can never finally remove racial distinctions. In No. 51 Madison contended that a well-constructed government will make use of passions to control passions. "Ambition must be used to counteract ambition."

Having three branches of government, our bicameral legislature, and an electoral college system, which mandates the need for candidates to seek to form coalitions among citizens of diverse States are the institutional expression of these aims for controlling factions from running rough-shod over majorities and minorities. But the question remains whether the Constitutional system and its realism actually make possible the kind of protection for Black interests for CRT advocates. We have noted Charles Lawrence's concern that racial prejudice disadvantages Black in this system in creating majorities with other factions to create a majority beneficial to Black Americans. Certainly, the Electoral College's decisive function in the Presidential elections of 1876, 1888, 2000, and 2016 has certainly not been to the advantage of African Americans in three cases, as they led to Rutherford Hayes' termination of Reconstruction, to the free-enterprise approach of George Bush's "Compassionate Conservatism," and to Donald Trump and his race-bashing. On the other hand, the results of 1888 did give America Benjamin Harrison who had fought in the Civil War for the Union and later sought (though unsuccessfully) to enhance voting rights for the freedmen in the South.

As for Madison's claim (in *The Federalist Papers*, No.10, see above) that in the Constitutional system, due to the difficulty of forming coalitions, there will not be much need for the government to protect minorities from the majority, Critical Race Theory may have a valid point in challenging that supposition. To the degree that Madison's supposition reflects the Constitutional system's biases, and in view of the history of white supremacy in our nation, CRT critiques of our Constitutional system seem validated. Let's explore that in closing this chapter, but first, we need to consider another element of the system about which CRT challenges have been issued.

We observed in the previous chapter CRT critiques of legal precedents and tacit consent on the grounds that these concepts effectively leave the assumptions of a racist society in place (see pp.17,19-20, above). And it is true that the Founders created a system based on tacit consent and so precedent. In so doing, they seem to have distanced themselves in The Constitution from the insights of John Locke more typical of The Declaration. While Locke presupposed a "Social Contract" (1690, 96-98), Thomas Reid (1751ff., 177), his American heirs claimed that if a government functions efficiently and legally, it does so only because a kind of contract between the people and rulers has been assumed – a kind of "tacit consent."

Reid's concept implies that once a government is in place, as long as its structures function efficiently and, presumably, in accord with natural law, then that government may validly impose its legal and constitutional judgments on the people, even if the majority would prefer at some point in history to reject such legislation or framed legislation contrary to constitutional provision. The Founders largely adopted this line of thinking. At least Madison reflected this view at the Constitutional Convention (p.393):

> A law violating a constitution established by the people themselves, would be considered by judges as null & void. 2. The doctrine laid down by the law of Nations in the case of treaties is that breach of one article by any of the parties, frees the other parties from engagements. In the case of a union of people under one Constitution, the nature of one pact has always been understood to exclude such an interpretation.

In a 1790 Letter to Thomas Jefferson, Madison expressly appealed to the concept of "tacit consent:"

> May it not be questioned whether it be possible to exclude wholly the idea of tacit consent, without subverting the foundation of civil Society? – on what principle does the voice of the majority bind the minority? It does not result I conceive from the Law of nature, but from compact

founded on conveniency... If this assent can not be given tacitly, or be not implied, where no positive evidence forbids, persons born in Society would not on attaining ripe age be bound by acts of the Majority, and either a *unanimous* repetition of every law would be necessary on the occasion of new members, or an express assent must be obtained from these to rule by which the voice of the Majority is made the voice of the whole.

It is clear that the perpetuity of the Constitution as well as the practice of judicial review by The Supreme Court reflects these commitments. For Constitutional roots of judicial review, see Art.III Sec.1 and Madison, 1787, pp.61,341. For the Constitution's intended perpetuity, its Purpose Statement is said to be to "establish Justice, insure domestic Tranquility, provide for the common defence, promote the general Welfare, and secure the Blessings of Liberty to ourselves and our **Posterity**." These commitments ensure that our Constitutional and judiciary system are not driven by a majority moved by the latest "sudden breeze of passion." Constitutional perpetuity and judicial precedent are in principle what protects the Black community from the latest and the next racist/nationalist majority wave. But only if the Constitution and the system it created are not themselves embedded in racism and white supremacy. It is time we looked again at all the statements in the document about slavery with which we began this chapter.

The Constitution and Slavery

If I have challenged the Right to this point, the next pages are a challenge to the Left (and yet I intend these points in the spirit of the Black community's long-term fidelity to The Constitution [Roberts, 1997, pp.1761-1762].) Of course The Constitution in its original form did not overtly condemn "America's original sin." But we need to examine why it was not condemned and why the Black man's status was identified as being just 3/5 that of a white's. Yes, political compromise looks ugly. However, is there any doubt that the Southern States would have failed to join the Union had slavery been abolished by the Founders (Robinson, p.88)? And the 3/5 rule was mostly driven by Northern State delegates as a way of reducing the Southern States' population and so would also reduce their political clout in the newly forming House of Representatives. In fact Southern States objected to reducing the value of slaves in determining the population of States (Madison, 1787, pp.259,274,281-282,285-286).

Regarding the allowing of the slave trade to continue twenty years after the adoption of the Constitution, a case might be made that once again this was dirty politics, a Northern States' ploy to ensure the Southern States' support of the document (see *Ibid.*, p.531). Rather than a pro-slavery move, it was a clause that at least James Wilson, a delegate to the Convention from Pennsylvania, believed would lay "the foundation for banishing slavery out of this country." ("Speech at Pennsylvania Ratifying Convention" [3 December 1787], in Kaminsky, p.463). James Madison, at least for purposes of advocating for The Constitution in *The Federalist Papers*, No.42, had a similar assessment about The Constitution's position on the slave trade. He wrote:

> It is doubtless wished that the power of prohibiting the importation of slaves had not been postponed until the year 1808, or rather that it had been suffered to have immediate operation... It ought to be considered as a great point gained in favor of humanity that a period of twenty years may terminate forever, within these States, a traffic which has so long and so loudly upbraided the barbarism of modern policy; that within that period it will receive considerable discouragement from the federal government, and may be totally abolished, by a concurrence of the few States which continue the unnatural traffic... Happy it would be for the unfortunate African if an equal prospect lay before them of being redeemed from the oppressions of their European brethren!

It should also be noted in connection with The Constitution's stricture on escape from service owed carefully avoids the words "slave" and "slavery." (see Madison, 1787, p.532), and his refusal to equate slavery with property; cf. (T. West, p.17). There is a lot of evidence to exonerate The Constitution from charges of being pro-slavery and favoring white supremacy.

These points could also be used against Derrick Bell's claim that The Bill of Rights aimed to protect slavery (esp. the Fifth Amendment and its clause that property cannot be taken for public use without due process and just compensation (1992, in Crenshaw et al., p.307). Nowhere in the Amendment nor anywhere in the entire Constitution is slavery designated as or associated with property.

Of course it could also be argued that The Constitution in effectively allowing for property ownership as a qualification for voting entailed establishing an oligarchy which excluded Blacks who owned disproportionately less property. But a careful reading of the document indicates that the Founders simply allowed States to determine who could vote in federal elections (Art. I, Sec.2). In that sense, The Constitution excludes no one from voting on the basis of wealth, gender, or race! And a case can be made that in the 1780s, when the document was drafted, significant numbers of Blacks and the poor were already voting. By the end of Washington's first term, only 4 of the 15 States in 1792 still had property qualifications (T. West, pp.113-114).

True enough, a number of Founders did have worries about giving everyone, even the poor, the right to vote. In Hamilton's 1775 treatise *Farmer Refuted* and in an 1829 Note made by Madison during the Convention for Amending the Constitution of Virginia both noted that the poor may not have opinions of their own, and could readily be manipulated by the rich who control their welfare. John Adams put it this way in a May 26, 1776 Letter:

> Men in general, in every society, who are wholly destitute of property, are also too little acquainted with public affairs to form a right judgment, and too dependent on other men to have a will of their own... [M]en who are wholly destitute of property... [are] to all intents and purpose as much dependent upon others, who will please to feed, clothe, and employ them, as women are upon their husbands, or children on their parents.

Though some of the members of the Constitutional Convention may have been intent on preserving slavery and a number owned slaves, we have other testimonies regarding the Founders' anti-slavery "original intent." Note Madison's 1787 "Speech at Pennsylvania Ratifying Convention" cited above. And in his speech on June 6 of that year to the Constitutional Convention, he stated that "we have seen the mere distinction of color made in the name of the most enlightened period of time, a ground of the most oppressive dominance every exercised by man over man." In an April 12, 1786, Letter to Gouverneur Morris, George Washington wrote that "There is not a man living who wishes more sincerely than I do to see a plan adopted to the abolition of it [slavery]." And as early as June 20, 1772, in a contribution to *The London Chronicle*, Benjamin Franklin wrote:

> It is to be wished that the same humanity [extended to a Black man named Sommersett] may extend itself among numbers; if not to the procuring liberty for those that remain in our Colonies, at least to obtain a law for abolishing the African commerce in Slaves, and declaring children of present Slavers free after they come of age. (in n.d., p.677)

On paper, there are certainly striking overlaps between the aims and realistic analyses of The Constitution and Critical Race Theory. But why then is structural racism around? And let us not overlook the critique of the Constitution's helpfulness to Black concerns by Neil Gotanda (in Crenshaw et al., esp.pp.257ff.), Alan Freeman, and other CRT advocates, including perhaps its primary inspiration, Nelson Bell (1992, in Crenshaw et al., pp.306-307). Why is it over the centuries that African Americans have maintained such faith in the Constitution as what can set them free (Nieman; Roberts, 1997, pp.1761ff.)?

Although he originally joined prominent white Abolitionist William Lloyd Garrison in critiquing the Constitution as pro-slavery, by 1860 the famed Black spokesman Frederick Douglass was ready to defend the value of the Constitution for the Black community ("Speech before the Scottish Anti-Slavery Society"). His points are still relevant for the dialogue with CRT and for all seeking fresh ways of liberation.

A Historic Black Model for Interpreting The Constitution

Douglass seeks to address the question of whether, as the Garrisonites contended, The Constitution is pro-slavery. Douglass clearly states that he denies that the Constitution guarantees a right to enslave other men. He hastens to add that the focus must be on what the document actually says, its "plain reading" and not on commentaries written about it. Likewise, with a hermeneutic at odds with Critical Race Theory (he alludes to common sense in his reading of the text, suggesting the influence of Common Sense Realism on him), he claims that

> It should also be borne in mind that the intentions of those who framed the Constitution, be they good or bad, for slavery or against slavery, are so respected so far, and so far only, as we find those intentions plainly stated in the Constitution. It would be the wildest of absurdities, and lead to endless confusion and mischiefs, if, instead of looking to the written paper itself, for its meaning, it were attempted to make us search out, in the secret motives, and dishonest intentions, of some of the men who took part in writing. It was what they said that was adopted by the people, not what they were ashamed or afraid to say, and really omitted to say.

In essence, Douglass believed that it does not matter that Washington, Jefferson, and Madison owned slaves. This neglect of the relevance of authorial intention and of the question about what a text means for today is certainly at odds with the critical models of interpretation suggested by CRT.

Douglass then proceeds with a careful analysis of the parts of the Constitution relevant to slavery. He notes that there are no direct references to "African slave trade" and "slave insurrections" appear in the text. Nowhere In the document is the colored man forbidden to vote.   The 3/5s clause regarding how to count African Americans in a State's populate is labeled as "a downright disability laid upon the slaveholding States." Regarding the clause pertaining to the eventual abolition of the slave trade (Art.1, Sec.9), the great emancipator notes that

The abolition of the slave trade was supposed to be the certain death of slavery. Cut off the stream and the pond will dry up, was the common notion at the time...it [this provision on slave trading] is anti-slavery, because it looked to the abolition of slavery rather than its perpetuity.

Regarding the provision concerning fugitive slaves and their recapture (Art. IV Sec.2), Douglass simply reiterates Madison's refusal to equate slaves with property that I have noted above (p.51). And in his response to the Constitution's reference to the so-called "slave insurrection clause" (Art. I Sec.8) he correctly notes that there is no reference to a slave rebellion in the text. But then he conceded that if the clause refers to slave insurrection, it left open the possibility that the President would be allowed under this clause to put down the insurrection by ending slavery. And so he concluded that the so-called slave-holding provisions of The Constitution are no guarantee of the perpetual defense of slavery!

But even if we grant these points, the CRT reminder of the persistence of white supremacy and The Constitutional system's role in permitting this seems to undercut the contemporary relevance of Douglass' point. In fact, he seems to have a defense from this critique, as his entire argument is framed by an important proviso. He urges that we not confound the reality of slavery during his time with the Constitution. The realities of slavery [racism] and The Constitution should not be "jumbled up." As he put it:

Thus, for instance, the American Government and the American Constitution are spoken of [by critics of the Constitution] in a manner which would naturally lead the hearer to believe that one is identical with the other; when the truth is, they are distinct in character as is a ship and a compass. The one may point right and the other steer wrong. A chart is one thing, the course of the vessel is another. The Constitution may be right, the Government wrong. If the Government has been governed by mean, sordid and wicked passions, it does not follow that the Constitution is mean, sordid and wicked.

Douglass clearly here explains why The Constitution can be deemed anti-racist while the judicial system it birthed and the government structures of America still reflect white supremacy. On Douglass' grounds, it seems that we might use The Constitution against traditions of interpretation or Constitutional precedents and against government institutions established under its auspices. Is this a way for CRT and its friends to continue to use the Constitution, highlighting its realist, common-sense suppositions, which they share in common, as a tool in the struggle against racism? Perhaps it could still be a valuable resource in seeking what Nelson Bell (1992, Crenshaw et al., p.306) terms new "racial strategies that can bring fulfillment and even triumph."

Overlooked Economic Aspects of Our Constitutional System: Would the Founders Support Reparations?

We have already noted that the Fifth Amendment of The Bill of Rights reflects the concern of many of the Founders to recognize a role for government in protecting property (see Alexander Hamilton, *The Federalist Papers*, Nos.17,54). But these rights are clearly subordinated to service to the common good. The Preamble only refers to "promoting the general Welfare," saying nothing about property protections, and where property is mentioned in the Fifth Amendment, a stipulation is made with due process that it could be taken for public use. Of course, this subordination of private property to the common good is embedded in the thinking of Thomas Reid and the Common Sense Realism which so influenced the Founders. Reid once wrote in *Practical Ethics* (p.208):

> In General as Property is introduced among Men for the Common Good it ought to be secure where it does not interfere with that end, but when that is the Case private Property ought to yield to Publick Good where there is repugnancy between them.

In a 1783 Letter to Robert Morris, Benjamin Franklin posited a similar subordination:

> All property, indeed, except the Savage's temporary Cabin, his Bow, his Matchcoat, ...seems to me to be the Creature of public Convention. Hence the Public has the Right of Regulating Descents, and all other Conveyances of Property, and even of limiting the Quantity and Uses of it. All the Property that is necessary to a Man, for the Consecration of the Individual and the Propagation of the Species, is his natural Right which none can justly deprive him of; But all Property superfluous to such purposes is the Property of the Publick, who may therefore by other Laws dispose of it, Whenever the Welfare of the Publick shall demand such Disposition.

Likewise, in the following order, Jefferson in a 1785 Letter To James Madison, Madison himself in a 1792 treatise on "parties," and Alexander Hamilton in No.58 of *The Federalist Papers* seem to opt for redistribution of property:

I am conscious that an equal division of property is impracticable, but the consequences of this enormous inequality producing so much misery to the bulk of mankind, legislators cannot invent too many devices for subdividing property, only taking care to let their subdivisions go hand in hand with the natural affectations of the human mind... Whenever there are in any country uncultivated lands and unemployed poor, it is clear that the laws of property have been so far extended as to violate natural right... If for the encouragement of industry we allow it [the land] to be appropriated, we must take care that other employment is provided to those excluded from appropriation.

Happy it is when the interest which the government has in the preservation of its own power coincide with a proper distribution of the public burdens and tend to guard the least wealthy part of the community from oppression.

[T]he great objection should be to combat the evil [of faction] by withholding *unnecessary* opportunities from a few... By the silent operation of laws, which without violating the rights of proper reduce extreme wealth towards a state of mediocrity, and raise extreme indigence towards a state of comfort.

Is the door not opened here for a vision of the Constitution in which laws and judicial review would be developed in relation to favorable outcomes for the Black community and all the impoverished?

In the CRT struggle to find new, effective racial strategies, the Constitution understood realistically seems like a valid tool, given all the points of contact – intersections. We have shown how The Constitution (as opposed to how it has been interpreted) endorses or makes possible the endorsement of all of CRT concerns and suppositions. We have seen that The Constitution offers a model for how to do politics, that we can get something done best by bringing together the various self-interested factions in American society in coalitions. In the next chapter, we will begin to observe similar points of contact between the CRT analysis and proposals and historic Christianity, see how a coalition between Christians of all races could be developed around the CRT agenda. And finally in the last chapter, we'll begin to examine how these coalitions could happen effectively.

Chapter 4

Christian Faith and Critical Race Theory: Some Surprising Compatibilities

Links between Critical Race Theory and Christian faith are no less profound and just as overlooked as the linkages between CRT and the U.S. Constitution. One point of contact with all sorts of implications for doing politics and changing America is implied in our discussion in the previous chapters regarding CRT's and the Constitution's collective cynicism about human nature, and the propensity of whites always to seek their own advantage. Even CRT's calls for Racial Realism and the recognition that white supremacy can never fully be overcome is a point of contact with historic Christian teaching. Christians have been making claims akin to these at least since the time of Augustine (354-430) and the development of the doctrine of Original Sin. Indeed, we have already shown that The Constitution's cynicism about human nature and what can be accomplished was indebted at least in part to Christian/Presbyterian sources.

Let's first get clear on what Original Sin is and how it relates to the CRT/Constitutional view of human beings and how we operate. Then, we can explore how the Christian remedies to our present state converge with CRT thinking and might be of use in furthering the aims of CRT and justice.

Original Sin

Rooted as they were in Jewish ways of perceiving the world, Christians did not (clearly) teach Original Sin in the first centuries. Rather, like Judaism, the earliest generation of post-Biblical Christians tended to define sin exclusively in terms of wrong actions, deeds that violate the Ten Commandments, with no reference to Original Sin (Clement of Rome, 38; Irenaeus, 27). The concept evolved gradually as the first Christian monks and nuns of Africa fled to the desert. The great saint Anthony (251-356), the most famous of the first of these monks, combined a strong doctrine of sin with the commitment to bear the Cross of Christ, but still affirmed our free will (Ward, pars.1,3,33). His colleagues in the desert were more radical in speaking of the hold sin has on us. Longinus and Matoes spoke of sin in terms of passions that overcome the soul. Moses the

Negro found an image to describe the sins that gripped him, noting that "sins run behind me, and I not see them..."

Earlier in the third century, a Bishop in North Africa named Commodianus had even identified sin with desire (64). The great champion of the Trinity doctrine, Athanasius (296-373), Bishop of Alexandria, who was himself a devoted advocate of the monks, continued in their tradition regarding the seriousness with which he took human sin. He spoke of the corruption caused by sin. On account of such sin, he contended, the human race was perishing and the image of God was disappearing in human beings as they became clouded by demoniacal deceit and insatiable sinning. Like the monks, though, Athanasius still affirmed human free will, a freedom to choose to avoid sin (5-7,13-14,54).

Previous to these developments, eminent theologians made comments suggestive of the doctrine of Original Sin as it later developed. Ancient North African theologian Tertullian (160-225) referred to Adam as "the originator of our race and our sin." Cyprian of Carthage (200-258) subsequently made affirmations about Baptism that were also pertinent to the development of the doctrine of Original Sin. In justifying the nascent practice of infant baptism he referred to the sin of infants in the sense of their having been "born of the fleshaccording to Adam," contracting "the contagion of ancient death." (64/58.5). These early theologians laid significant groundwork for understanding sin as something bigger than the individual and personal misdeeds, but as a reality or condition which infects our entire nature, even our institutions, from birth.

Biblical Roots

Of course, there are Biblical precedents for these affirmations. The Old Testament or Hebrew Bible has many express references to "sins" against the Commandments and the Law of God. And the four Gospels of the Christian New Testament continued to refer to sins in this tradition. However, at an early stage in the development of these Old Testament texts, sins came to be related not just to misdeeds but also to a lack of faith (Exodus 32; esp. v.21).

The Genesis 3 account of the Fall of Adam and Eve became a crucial text for the Christian doctrine of Sin. Although Jewish leaders did not understand the Fall in this way, New Testament writers began to speak of the transmission of sin to all human beings through Adam (Romans 5:12-14; 1 Corinthians 15:22). Psalms 51:5 ("I was... a sinner when my mother conceived me") can be cited in support of this idea that one is born in sin by virtue of the Fall.

Other Biblical texts are pertinent for establishing the pervasive character of sin, that it is more than mere misdeeds and is instead a reality that saturates the whole of human nature. Romans 7 (esp. vv.14-23) portrays sin as a reality that forces human beings to do and to will what they otherwise would not want to.

Ecclesiastes 4:4 also seems relevant. The text reads: "Then I saw that all labor and all skill in work come from one person's envy of another. This also is vanity and a striving after wind." The text suggests that every dimension of human activity is the result of envy and the desire to get ahead of one's neighbor (i.e., the result of competition and concupiscence).

The Augustinian Synthesis

The occasion for gathering up these insights into a fully developed doctrine of Original Sin in which all sins are said to be rooted was a famous controversy between Augustine and Pelagius (approx. 360-420), a devout monk from Britain (perhaps Ireland). Fervently pious, the monk despaired of the lukewarm Christianity that seemed to plague his contemporaries. His response was to teach and preach a rigid moralism. Christian life, in Pelagius' view, was all about the effort to overcome sins in order to attain salvation. This required a belief that people have complete freedom to choose whether to sin or not to sin.

Pealgius' debate with Augustine was occasioned by the African Father's prayer in his classic work *The Confessions* (X.XXXIX.40): "Give what Thou command and command what Thou wilt." Pelagius rejected the idea that God commands the impossible, as Augustine seemed to imply (16). The two contemporaries would be locked in a heated debate for years, with Augustine's side eventually prevailing.

The African Father's primary agenda was not to lament the power of sin, but to assert the primacy of God's action and forgiving love, to confess that Christ is humanity's only hope. Pelagius' portrait of how we are saved and what human beings can accomplish contradicted this Augustinian vision. If we are not totally immersed in sin, then it logically follows that we can save ourselves, that we can achieve the good life on our own.

In addition to these commitments, Augustine's own life had revealed to him the hopelessness of the human condition in sin (399, X.XXVIII.39). So bound to sin are we, he insisted (in the spirit of Romans 7), that when it comes to avoiding sin we have no free will. Without the grace of God we cannot stop sinning (412, III.5).

If we have free will and can in principle choose the good, we open the door again to the possibility that we can overcome sin and save ourselves. Consequently, our total dependence on God is at stake in these commitments (see Romans 3:21-28; Galatians 3:1-14).

Our bondage to sin does not necessarily mean that we are reduced to robots. It is theologically appropriate to continue to assert our freedom to choose actions without compromising the claim that we are in bondage to sin. For example, readers are free to decide whether to continue reading this book or whether to discontinue reading. On Augustine's grounds and most compatible with the findings of modern research on the brain, either way, you are sinning, because the decision made in each case is self-serving (doing what makes you feel good). Likewise, in the political realm, one is free to support the free market or to opt for a managed economy with Affirmative Action policies, but either way, it is self-interest which drives these choices (the very suppositions we observed in the last chapter, which underlie our Constitutional system of government). CRT thinkers are correct from a Christian point of view. Even when whites (and Blacks) do the right thing on race issues, practice justice, they are still driven by their own interests.

The first Protestant Reformer was in line with this way of thinking. He spoke of the inescapability of sin with the Latin phrase *in curvatus in se* (curved in on ourselves) (1515-1516, in WA56:304). More important for the American scene, John Calvin spoke of blind self-love innate in all human beings (II.I.1-2). All of us are always seeking ourselves and what is good for us.

Sin As Concupiscence

The next challenge faced by Augustine was how unequivocally to assert our bondage to sin. The weight of precedent and how the Biblical witness had been interpreted in previous centuries moved him to talk about sin as something we are born with and to depict in terms of desire or lust (399, VI.XV.25; XIII.VII.8). Certainly, when someone is lusting (be it a sexual lust or a lust for power) that person is in bondage to that person or thing. You cannot make many free decisions in the heat of passion. You just do what the lust demands.

Augustine described this bondage to lust as concupiscence, designating it as "the law of sin" (418/420, I.XXI.24 – I.XXIII.25). *Concupiscence*, of course, is a term referring to a strong, compelling desire, especially like sexual lust. By employing this term, which had strong autobiographical significance for him based on his youthful sexual adventures, the African Father was provided with a powerful way of expressing the bondage of sin without reducing human beings to the status of mere robots. Just as one cannot stop a sexual encounter in the heat of passion, so sinners seeking their own gratification cannot stop seeking their own self-interest, even when they know better that the right thing is to aid your poor neighbor in need. It is as St. Paul said in Romans 7:15 and 19: "I do not understand my own actions. For I do not do the good as I want, but I do the very thing I hate... For I do not do the good I want, but the evil I do not want is what I do."

Augustine conceives of fallen human beings as addicts. Like sex addicts, the more we are driven to seek pleasure and self-fulfillment, the less we will be satisfied, and so the more pleasures we will need to seek. The more you desire, the more you sin, and the more you sin, the more you desire. The African Father more or less made this point when he claimed that (human) nature and custom (or actions) join together to render cupidity strong (396/398, I.I.10). Among the first Protestants, not just Martin Luther (1517, in WA1:255) but also John Calvin (II.I.8) described sin in terms of concupiscence. This analysis of human nature makes clear why the white establishment in America wants more and more, feels tugged to keep a permanent underclass, and so even why the system we have created keeps working to maintain white privilege. Critical Race Theory is certainly not teaching anything which is contrary to Christian faith at this point, is it?

It would be a mistake to understand Augustine or his Protestant Reformation heirs to be defining sin merely as lustful actions that result in visible violations of the Ten Commandments and of expectations of good citizenship in a society. His point in describing sin as concupiscence was to make clear that *all* human deeds, even those outwardly good, are sinful. Augustine did believe that sinful human beings are capable of outwardly good deeds. Indeed, such acts are no less outwardly good than deeds motivated by the love of God. He even claimed that the works of pride (concupiscence) are akin to those of love. Both can feed the hungry and care for the dying. The difference is that love does what it does for God in Christ, while pride does what it does in order to gain some glory (ca.417, VIII.9).

Martin Luther made a similar point, claiming "For man cannot but seek his own advantages and love himself above all things... Hence even in good things and virtues men seek themselves, that is they seek to please themselves... I say now no one should doubt that all out good works are mortal sins..." (1515-1516, in WA56:237). Nothing human beings do or touch is tainted by our concupiscent desires for power and self-interest. John Calvin, who, as we've noted has had more direct influence on America's political structures, said much the same thing in teaching "total depravity" (I.I.2).

In the previous chapter we noted how a number of America's Founders, those responsible for the Constitution, no doubt influenced by John Calvin's similar assessment of human nature, understood human beings in terms of this critical assessment of human nature. If you agree, it should come as no surprise to anyone, including proponents of Critical Race Theory, that white Liberal support of Civil Rights was and continues to be in the self-interests of these whites. Everything that fallen human beings do is ultimately driven by the burning desire to please the ego. Even the good deeds that I do are scarred by my egocentric desires to do good. In order to get more out of the white community, to get more support for Civil Rights as defined by Critical Race Theory, it's going to take efforts to show these potential allies that dismantling white privilege is more in their interests than preserving the present (white-privileged) meritocracy. The final segments of this chapter and the rest of this book will provide some arguments for and strategies to do so. Christian faith and insights from modern science help.

First, though, let's be very sure that the full implications of this Augustinian version of Original Sin are clear. There is a sense in which, on his grounds, the behavior of Mother Teresa and Martin Luther King Jr. was no better than that of Hitler and the Jan. 6 rioters. All were driven in some sense by the lust for power and influence (concupiscence). Before God, they and we stand equally condemned unless the miracle of God's love intervenes.

Augustine tried to explain how the sinful condition is inescapable. He basically affirmed that Original Sin and concupiscence are transmitted in the sex act. Good sex involves concupiscence, and so the product of the sexual union (the fetus and so the human being thus created) as the product of concupiscence is itself concupiscent from birth (418/420, LXXIV.27). A distinct twentieth-century version of this way of thinking has been identified by the eminent Swiss Reformed theologian Karl Barth, whose thinking is in line with Critical Race Theory's inclination to see racism as a social construct. For Barth, sin is essentially the result of how society functions (Vol.IV/1, p.492). In his view, human beings are what they do or what is done to them. For example, Mark Ellingsen is nothing more than the sum total of all things he has done and has happened to him. Given the Barthian scheme, we can observe that just as Mark Ellingsen and the readers of this volume have been exposed only to concupiscent human beings (except to Jesus Christ) their whole lives, it is hardly surprising that the nature formed by such encounters would wind up being concupiscent.

The observations that Critical Race Theory makes about how racism is shaped by social structures is right in line with such thinking. A society given birth by white supremacy structures its social institutions and laws that way. And so it inevitably replicates in white racism unless or until you racially change the structures in favor of those not privileged and getting the shaft. If you don't like Critical Race Theory for making those points, better reject Christianity too (at least stop teaching Original Sin). Of course, as we've already noted, a lot of this line of thinking is also implied in the American Constitutional system.

How Such Thinking Got Into the American Political System

The presence of these Christian elements in our political system is largely overlooked in our public school system and in a lot of scholarship. We hear much of the influence of Enlightenment scholars like John Locke or Lord Montesquieu. And we never hear of Rev. John Witherspoon, the favorite teacher of James Madison at Princeton University or about how Witherspoon and Jefferson were influenced by a philosophy called Scottish Common Sense

Realism. A study conducted by University of Houston Professor of Political Philosophy Donald S. Lutz found that in documents written by the 55 men who wrote the U.S. Constitution, 34% of their direct quotes were drawn from the Bible, while only 8.3% came from the writings of Montesquieu and 2.9% by Locke. We have already noted the evidence in the writings of Thomas Jefferson of the influence of the Scottish Common Sense philosophy on him and on many American colleges and universities of the late Colonial era (1771; 1824). And we have observed that James Madison noted the great influence John Witherspoon had on him (1769).

Likewise, in the previous chapter we noted how these commitments led the Founders to opt for a government structure reflecting the separation of powers and a check-and-balance system. Recall Witherspoon, working out of his Calvinist/Presbyterian commitments, opted for a model of government which prefigures the Constitutional model of his student Madison (1774, p.144).

Some of the greatest American Christian social thinkers of the past century have opted for viewing society in terms of Original Sin and the realism about politics which goes with it. We have already noted in passing Critical Race Theory's assessment of Martin Luther King, Jr. Along with the famed Christian Social Ethicist Reinhold Niebuhr (a major player in mid-century liberal Democratic politics) King referred to the complexity of human motives (an allusion to Critical Race Theory's idea of interest convergences) and sin (1960).

This kind of realism about human nature leads to a realism about what social reforms can accomplish. We've already noted how Critical Race Theory leaders seem to endorse King's idea that the struggle to actualize his idea of the beloved community in history might not ever be fully realized. But you still have to struggle to actualize the ideal if you want to transform society. And likewise the primary allies in this realism about human nature on account of Original Sin would say the same thing. Thus Augustine taught that an unambiguously just peace was impossible to achieve because we will always seek to impose our version of peace on others. True justice has no existence in the earthly city (413-426, XIX.12; II.21).

This description is certainly in line with the dynamics which have led to white supremacy. As such, it is another example of the compatibility between CRT's analysis of political realities and the views of historical Christianity and our Constitutional system. In this connection, the views of the first great Protestant Martin Luther are a further illustration of historic Christianity's realism about the role and government and why we need it. Thus, he claimed that we need government in order to avoid blood baths, but he in turn insisted that no Christian government is possible as coercion is necessary for it to function (1525, in WA18: 306,327; 1535-1545, in WA42:79).

Biochemistry and Genetics

The apparent common sense of these Christian insights (much too pessimistic for significant segments of happy, well-adjusted white and Black Americans) is rooted in scientific findings, it seems. We all know of the role of genes in making us who we are. It seems that the human bodies function to maximize reproduction of DNA (the carrier of genetic information). As a result, because of the struggle to survive, universal love and welfare of the species as a whole do not make evolutionary sense. These dynamics have led researcher Richard Dawkins to refer to the "selfish gene." His theory certainly appears to explain kin selection – why parents love their children and why members of ethnic groups tend to prefer their own and guard each other's welfare over outsiders. These Geneological insights seem to verify the Augustinian-Pauline concept of sin as egocentricity, which I've been discussing. Add to this the insights of Neurobiology.

The study of the human brain has revealed that it develops from back to front. It is the front part of our brains which distinguishes humans from the rest of the animal world. This section, called the frontal lobe, controls important cognitive functions and voluntary movement. Its frontal cortex is essentially the executive portion of the brain, managing input from and directing all the other lobes. When functioning efficiently it manages systems in the brain responsible for emotions and memory.

It is essential, then, that this part of the brain has connections with other parts of the brain. Making these connections is assisted by certain brain chemicals called monoamines. The release of these brain chemicals is triggered by the electrical impulses caused by neural dendrites (branched projections from the brain fibers, connecting with other brain fibers and their cells). This brain cells connect to each other which binds them. And the chemicals facilitating the process are experienced as pleasurable, for they are amphetamine-like chemicals called dopamine. This monoamine flows in higher quantity when the prefrontal cortex is exercised. And that part of our brains is exercised in the higher human activities controlling our emotions, like love, friendship, social engagement, reading, writing, spirituality, engaging in art and music, etc. Not only is it pleasurable, but as associated with these higher brain functions, it seems to stimulate these activities as well. Dopamine also gives the body more energy and seems to stimulate the production of more antibodies. In short, it is good for your health.

Another brain chemical released in such activities (notably in nurturing) is oxytocin. It affects not only muscle compatibility in order to facilitate sperm and egg transport but also increases feelings of love and empathy as it calms the brain and makes one want to cuddle with the object of affection. It too both feels good and renders one more sociable and caring.

The takeaway from these observations is that even in the highest activities of human beings, when we love, nurture, do justice, create, and even pray, we are still selfish sons of guns. These activities feel good. Neurobiology and Genetic Research both provide supporting evidence in favor of the Christian view of Original Sin. And as such, they also seem to verify the analysis of America's Founders regarding factions of the self-interested character of all that human beings do. The American political system may have lasted as long and as well as it has because it has built in some safeguards to counter and redirect these very human propensities.

These observations have implications for the views of Critical Race Theory. Its proponents caution that white interests were being met by desegregation and support of the Civil Rights Movement have not just Christian but also scientific support. A version of history which did not teach this would run counter to Scientific findings. Critics of teaching these perspectives in our schools seem not to have a leg to stand on, if they want to trust the Science and (if Christian) be in line with their own faith commitments. But on the other hand, Critical Race Theory then needs to come to terms with the fact that its agenda and proposals are also in the self-interests of the African-American community (a concession which seems made). And also, the fact that white interests being met when racism is challenged might be seen not so much as a critique, but as a reality with which to reckon if white supremacy is ever to be curtailed. In other words, these scientific and Christian insights prod proponents of Critical Race Theory "to think smart," to find arguments and ways to allure the (still) white majority and its power-brokers to see that in ending white privilege, there might be something in it for them. The rest of this chapter and this book suggests some possibilities. Again, we find some surprising compatibilities between the aims of Christian faith and CRT.

The Christian Vision and the King Dream

We have already noted how some proponents of Critical Race Theory find Martin Luther King's image of the "beloved community" compelling, a goal, though not realizable in history (Cook, 1991; see King, 1956). This is the image of a community characterized by cooperation, friendship, and understanding among all parts of a diverse community, a community without poverty and discrimination. No place for white supremacy in such a community.

If we keep in mind King's Augustinian view of sinful human nature, his realism about achieving complete racial harmony, then the differences between him and CRT realism are not so great (1968, in 1986, p.277; 1960, pp.439-440). Even CRT proponent Anthony Cook (Crenshaw et al., pp.96-97) and Kimberlé Crenshaw (2022) seem to recognize these convergences.

Of course, it has been noted by Brandon Paradise, a Law Professor at Rutgers University (pp.116ff.) that CRT has largely marginalized Christian thought. And Paradise (p.189) contends that even though Cook placed CRT in dialogue with King's thinking, he missed King's realism, falsely accusing him at first of relying on an optimistic view of human nature to authorize the Civil Rights leader's image of a "beloved community (King, 1957). Cook is also critiqued by Paradise (pp.192ff.) for claiming, when he finally acknowledges King's realism about human nature, that this critique of human nature and society is a function of his use of DeConstruction like CRT and Critical Legal Studies employ. In fact, King himself (1960, pp.439-441) noted his indebtedness about realism to a spiritual heir of Augustine, the famed modern Social Ethicist Reinhold Niebuhr.

Even the reflections on CRT relations to King offered by Kimberlé Crenshaw fall short in the same respects regarding her understanding of why King holds views like CRT. She is absolutely correct in contending that, like CRT, he recognized the structural character of racism, that institutions need to be changed if justice is to be achieved. But she too fails to recognize that King held thesCRT convictions because of his faith commitments (the Augustinian view of sin).

Both Cook and Crenshaw do not fully explore CRT links to King and Christian faith regarding constructively what the Black community might do in seeking alternatives to whitesupremacy (see Paradise, pp.204-2106). Paradise notes that there is some reference in Cook's work to transformation as playing a role in King's thought and how it might relate the Postmodern concern to taking new orientations to the worldview of others, but the point is not developed or explicitly applied to strategies for building coalitions with American factions like I will in the Conclusion.

In any case, we can say clearly that Dr. King's reflections and dreams, along with his skepticism about their full realization, are most compatible with the Christian faith's answers to the mess we are in. Although church structures have too infrequently embodied this faith commitment, the Christian Word of God teaches that ultimately ethnic differences do not matter. It is as St. Paul once wrote: "There is no longer Jew or Greek, there is no longer slave or free, there is no longer male and female; for all of you are one in Christ Jesus." (Galatians 3:28) Critical Race Theory's insights about the fact that racial differences are more about social condition than genetics seem vindicated in this Biblical testimony. Christian faith supports this legal theory in another way. As CRT advocates call for examining laws in light of the condition of the Black community and those victimized, so Jesus in His Ministry and the early Christians seem to have been preoccupied with the poor, showing them a preference in outreach to and care for them (Mark 10:21; Luke 4:18; Galatians 2:10; James 2:15).

At this point, however, we cannot make these faith commitments about Jesus to be the intellectual or political reason for seeking to restructure American institutions to the benefit of the poor and oppressed. To do so would be in violation of the First Amendment. Far better to make the case for a society not based on white supremacy by appealing to the Founders' suppositions observed in the previous chapter regarding the need for a government in which property serves the people (see quotations in p.55). But it seems that Christians with faith principles rooted in a preference for the poor will be motivated to take up this task, that their vision will not be so different from those which CRT aims to achieve.

Of course Black Liberation Theology, a spiritual heir of Dr. King, contends that Christianity teaches a preferential option for the poor (Cone, 1985: 755-756,768-769). These commitments have ancient theological roots, dating back to the early centuries of the Church, in Clement of Alexandria (II.XIII), who once wrote:

> God brought our race into communion by first imparting what was His own, when He gave His own Word, common to all, and made all things for all. All things, therefore are common, and not for the right to appropriate an undue share.

Clement's words are certainly in line with the safety-net images for the poor found in comments we noted by America's Founders and also reflects CRT concerns to focus on the well-being of those victimized by racism. Centuries later, St. Augustine while praying (in his *Confesisons*, XIII.18) urged God to "Let us break bread with the hungry and bring into our own house the needy and those with no home.. to clothe the naked." Martin Luther, the first Protestant Reformer opted for a similar role for government. He wrote (in *The Large Catechism*, I.7):

> To restrain open lawlessness is the responsibility of princes and magistrates. They should be alert and resolute to establish and maintain order in all areas of trade and commerce in order the poor may not be burdened and oppressed.

In Luther's view (continuing today in most of the Lutheran nations of Europe), government should manage the economy in the interests of the poor. In the twentieth century, Reinhold Niebuhr, who as we have noted, influenced Dr. King, said much the same about government management:

> The sharpening of class antagonism within each modern industrial nation is increasingly destroying national unity and imperiling

international comity as well. It may be that the constant growth of economic inequality and social injustice in our industrial civilization will force the nations into a final conflict... the disintegration of national loyalties through class antagonisms has proceeded so far in the more advanced nations, that they can hardly dare to permit the logic inherent in the present situation to take its course. Conditions in these nations,... reveal what desperate devices are necessary for the preservation of even a semblance of national unity... (1932)

CRT clearly aligns with Christian faith on this matter.

Insights from Biology and the Human Genome Project in particular also support Critical Race Theory's contention that racial differences are more about social condition than genetics. Indeed, modern insights from the field of Evolution along with Neurobiology are also found to support this sense of human harmony as new research suggests that the human cooperative propensities are what account for the success of the human race. Of course, something like that has been taught for nearly 2 millennia by the Christian faith. But let's talk a little more about these findings, as they not only further vindicate Critical Race Theory. These insights also provide insight into the kind of self-interest those with power and privilege might have in renouncing some of their existing privilege.

Dialogue with Evolution and Brain Research

Christians believe that Paul's and King's vision of what God plans to do with us is in line with God's original intention for humankind, that it is a new creation (2 Corinthians 5:17). And so it follows that we can learn more about what this vision entails from looking at the beginning of life. New insights emerging from the Theory of Evolution are most valuable in fleshing out this vision and what Critical Race Theory wants.

Evolution teaches us that in order to understand the human species you need to recognize its relation to its ancestral environment. Throughout recorded history and even in prehistoric times, we have always been surrounded either by homo sapiens or by hominoid predecessors. Evidence suggests that in order to account for all the genetic variants in homo sapiens, given mutation rates and the length of homo sapiens' existence (at most, not more than 200.000 years), we must have evolved from a population of about 7000 in Africa (Tenesa, Navarro, et al., pp. 520-526). In short, human beings have always been in community with other human beings! And since all these homos sapiens were themselves enmeshed in a community, we can assume that throughout our evolutionary history, we have been hanging out with others who were cooperative people in close-knit groups (D. Wilson, pp.151-153).

We are a cooperative species evolving from cooperative forebears. This is born out by Archeology and Genetic Biology. It is a finding which can help account for the size of our brains, for the larger brains we have are functions of our more fully developed frontal lobes homo sapiens have developed which control our animal instincts and selfishness. Even Albert Einstein, himself an enemy of racism, also understood Physics to entail our cooperative nature as he claimed that all true religion aims to overcome the optical delusion of our consciousness that we are separate from the universe.

To be sure, other species cooperate. Birds, bees, and many animals, for example. However, much animal cooperation is a function of sharing a common gene pool. Though perhaps not at the earliest stages of human evolution, modern homo sapiens are distinct in their ability to cooperate in large communities, even among those who do not share many common genes (Harari). Consider how much driving on the highways and America's city streets involves high levels of cooperation, how cooperation transpires in a big business or nation, and even more so in the globalized forms of economic cooperation! Homo sapiens' ability to cooperate is amazing.

Christianity of course has historically affirmed this. Thus, Pope John Paul II, during his reign, spoke of the social love and solidarity among human beings (32-33). And Martin Luther King, Jr. observed that "We are all caught in an inescapable network of mutuality... We are made to live together because of the interrelated structure of reality (1986, p.254). Physics and the Christian faith teach us that humans are at their best when they are cooperating. Indeed, further Evolutionary studies suggest that such cooperation may be at the heart of religion, and so its practice might contribute to the aims of Critical Race Theory.

Recently, students of Evolutionary Theory have applied this research to Religious Studies. Anthropologists and Biologists have observed that religion may have given homo sapiens an advantage in nurturing cooperation. The gods which were served were construed as omniscient and could punish selfishness and misdeeds. Religion spiritualizes cooperative behavior, providing a supernatural incentive for practicing behavior which restricts selfishness (Rossano, pp.174-177; Wade, pp.55-56). It also cultivates trust among adherents essential for cooperation. Even patterned worship, when it takes the form of dancing or bodily movements like standing, sitting, kneeling, and singing (as transpires in many churches and mosques) can provide a sense of group cohesion among the faithful (Wade, pp.79-81,198ff.). People involved in these sorts of belief structures and worship will have their natural sense of or desire for collaboration so strengthened that it becomes less and less desirable for such individuals to want to work alone or to dominate others.

The contribution world religions (those whose membership transcends an ethnic group) can make to human collaboration, and so to fighting racism and white supremacy, is also verified by research on the human brain. It seems that spirituality exercises the front part of our brains, the prefrontal cortex (which as we have noted has executive functions in controlling emotions and our other perceptions). It is the part of the brain active in the functions which we would consider most uniquely human (like love, care, and creativity) (Wade, p.22; Newberg and Waldman, pp.42ff.). In other words, the very parts of the brain stimulated by spiritual experiences are the brain functions and are what make homo sapiens distinct and uniquely capable of cooperation. Besides the activations of the frontal cortex, it seems that spirituality also stimulates the brain's anterior cingulate cortex. This cortex is the part of the brain situated between the frontal lobe and the limbic system, which contains the brain's emotional circuits. The anterior cingulate cortex mediates these thoughts and feelings. It is crucial for social awareness and empathy. Religious experience, then, enhances empathy and social awareness (Newberg, pp.52-53). Again, it is evident how religion enhances our cooperative abilities. It seems plausible to conclude, then, that religion has contributed to human evolution, helped make us the creatures we are. To the degree that Critical Race Theory's aims in abolishing racism and white supremacy parallel the brain dynamics of faith, we might be enabled to make the case that renunciation of white supremacy is not only in line with Christian faith but makes us more human. Would that be an appeal to self-interest which CRT might use in seeking actually to achieve its aims? Renouncing white privilege makes us all (Black, white, Asian, and indigenous) more human.

Another way in which religion in general and Christian faith in particular enhances morality and cooperation with the other relates to the brain chemical secreted in spiritual exercises. As we previously noted, our use of the frontal cortex is rewarded and its repeated use is encouraged by the secretion of pleasurable brain chemicals, dopamine and oxytocin (*Ibid.*, pp.55-56). And these brain chemicals also enhance or are associated with bonding and so with sociality.

Of course, qualifications drawn from the insights of Critical Race Theory and even from Christian faith need to be made about how useful these brain chemicals may be in the struggle with racism. Let's not forget CRT's racial realism, that full equality will not happen given our present system's biases. And Christian faith is even more radical, contending that on this side of Christ's Second coming we will never be without sin, that absolute cooperation never transpires perfectly. Those who claim that CRT violates Christian faith in contending that racism will ever plague us, that all whites profiting from the system are racists, clearly misunderstand the doctrine of Original Sin. The possibility of repentance by all is not being denied by CRT. You can always become anti-racist, commit to fighting it. But even then, you are still a sinner ensconced in racism.

To be sure, dopamine leads to repentant activity, makes you more inclined to be social. But oxytocin can bias you to be kinder to those of your own kin (perhaps explaining why in the name of religion many have been killed). This is a caution to remind us that religion alone will not heal the nation's wounds or rid of white supremacy. We need laws and the Constitution's check-and-balance system functioning optimally and justly to check our natural (sinful) inclinations to favor those of our own kind. And even The Constitution's Founders conceded that there were "bugs in the machine" they created (see Conclusion). Evolution does not guarantee that our cooperation will ever be seemless. We have that instinct as humans, but nothing guarantees that it will be realized in any particular setting or that it might be realized only through the suppression of others. Our cooperation is an evolving process. Of course, Dr. King's image of the beloved community and St. Paul's reminders that we are all one (Romans 12:4-5; 1 Corinthians 10:17; 12:12ff.; Galatians 3:28), along with our natural cooperative inclinations are helpful antidotes for overcoming our ethnocentrism.

It is obvious that religion provides incentives and rewards for abolishing barriers to cooperation like racism and white supremacy. Given our natural human propensity towards cooperation, the practice of faith and with it, the rejection of racism make us more fully human, as well as both happier and healthier. Christianity, along with Evolution and Neurobiology, offer the incentives to practice the agenda of Critical Race Theory. Ending racism and white supremacy is ultimately good for everybody, even for white folks. Why practice white supremacy and racism since they make you less human and don't get you the good brain dope which makes you happier? Proponents of Critical Race Theory, Civil Rights initiatives as a whole, would do well to get this message out. More on this in the Conclusion.

Storytelling

Another point of connection between Christian faith and Critical Race Theory is to be found in their shared commitment to story-telling. We have already noted CRT's reliance on this approach as a means of communicating to the public the challenges and pains encountered by Black men and women. Of course, this commitment is in line with the heritage of African-American culture and its church (Banks: 410ff.). But this has also been part of the heritage of large segments of Christianity, dating back to the character of large segments of the Hebrew Bible and the Gospels as stories. Historians believe such communication through narrative dominated in Western Christianity at least through the eighteenth century (Frei, p.1). The convergence has another significant characteristic that I want to explore in closing comments in this chapter.

It seems that the use of narratives and story-telling facilitates understanding. MRI research on the human brain undertaken by some Princeton University researchers discovered that the brain activity of one listening to a story mirrors the speaker's brain activity with a delay. In other words, the brain areas activated by the story in the listener are precisely what the brain activity is of the speaker of the words (Stephens, Silbert, and Hasson: 4425-14430). Stories or narratives clearly communicate the message that both Critical Race Theory and Christian faith want to communicate. This insight undermines the critiques of those who have chided CRT proponents for swapping stories for objective analysis. In fact, the use of stories to communicate, like CRT and historic Christianity advocates is the best medium for communicating objective, descriptive truth which can cross ethnic lines.

The facts presented in this chapter and the previous one indicate that Critical Race Theory is not so subversive after all. Not only do its findings and aims line up with the U.S. Constitution. But many of its suppositions connect with the Christian faith, and most other religions found in America. However, on the other hand, the data presented in this chapter in particular does raise a challenge to CRT which demands attention.

Can Critical Race Theory Endorse and Be Helped by Objectivity? How Faith and Evolution Might Help

The findings discerned from how story-telling enhances communication as well as the insights gained from both Christian faith and Evolution, suggest that we can communicate across ethnic and genetic lines. Recall that Critical Race Theory opts for a Standpoint Epistemology. This entails that each person or group has a unique point of view in interpreting texts and laws. This is the position of all the leading Philosophical influences on CRT. I have challenges to this commitment in view of the evidence we have been considering regarding the racist origins of standpoint, critical epistemology in Kant as well as with an eye towards what Critical Race Theory aims to accomplish.

CRT advocates have been correct to challenge "accepted truths," including the "objectivity" of the present American legal system and how it reflects the interests of white privilege. But if we can never agree across racial/ethnic lines, is real cooperation possible? Trans-racial cooperation demands that we can truly be open when communicating with each other. The Christian vision of there being neither Greek nor Jew, slave nor free, prods us away from believing we cannot understand each other. And the neurobiological research on storytelling as a resource in furthering communication has shown that those sharing a story, no matter their ethnicity, even share similar brain patterns.

Another scientific and Christian insight challenges the subjectivism of Critical Race Theory. The brain mechanisms of morality, embedded as they are in the prefrontal lobes of the human brain, seems similar among all human beings. And so we might reasonably conclude that, despite the marked differences in cultural expressions, human beings think about morality in similar ways. Christians and other religious people and Philosophers call this the natural law, the belief that the nature of right and wrong is accessible to all through reason (Romans 2:14-15). And this concept is presupposed in both The Declaration of Independence (expressly referring to "the laws of nature") and in The U.S. Constitution's Bill of Rights. Recent Anthropological research has even begun to corroborate this common morality. An Oxford University study of 60 societies found that they all shared a common set of rubrics regarding helping kin, reciprocat- ing, deferring to superiors, and the like, behaviors that promote cooperation (Curry, Mullins, and Whitehouse).

The Christian belief and Evolutionary/Anthropological findings that we can discern a common morality clearly represent an amendment of Critical Race Theory's position, one which might render it more effective in accomplishing its aims. Positing the possibility that we can share common principles across racial/ethnic lines would offer the possibility of gaining broader public support, as then whites and others would not feel excluded from the CRT agenda but could more readily feel they could get on board with such an agenda. Christian insights (especially the call to appeal to a common morality [natural law] like America's Founders did, along with the hopefulness about the future the Christian faith brings) might offer a model for building the sort of coalitions it will take to overcome racism in American society.

None of this is intended to neglect CRT warnings about white supremacy and how it will not be curtailed simply through Constitutional principles of equal rights. We need to "get real" on that point. But we also need to recognize that building coalitions with whites in order to make gains will require cultivating white interests to intersect with Black causes. That will require communication across racial/cultural lines, and perhaps the CRT Postmodern Standpoint Epistemology does not make this possible. In fact, these commitments could be a barrier to cooperation if we cannot communicate across racial lines. Indeed, adopting a mode of interpretation in line with Frederick Douglass' approach to The Constitution (see Chapter Three) has more roots in grassroots Black culture which is (to use CRT modes of thought) more "Modern or Pre-Modern than does CRT "Postmodernity." And Douglass' sort of interpretive model if rigorously applied also has a better chance of critiquing the "indeterminacy of legal doctrine" which worried CRT scholars. For while on CRT grounds it is not readily possible, Douglass' model leaves out the hope that we can demonstrate how some things in the Constitution do not allow for racial discrimination, a safety net you lose if all statements have only indeterminate meaning. If CRT is correct, it is a little easier for whites to do their racist supremacy thing with the Constitution.

What's in It for All of Us?

The Christian and Evolutionary insight about how we are creatures designed to cooperate is a promising direction for beginning to give Critical Race Theory what it demands. My proposal is made in the spirit of both Douglass along with the realism of CRT and St. Augustine. No time for white supremacy in the midst of true cooperation. In this chapter, we've been answering what's in it for whites, for as we have seen both CRT and American's Founders recognized that in order to move things politically there must be something in it for all factions. The data noted in this chapter indicate that when white privilege and racism are overcome, barriers to being who we truly are (cooperative organisms) begin to whither. And we have also noted that then the good brain chemicals (oxtyocin and dopamine) which are secreted in our brains when we forget ourselves, practice morality, and live in social dialogue with our neighbors will begin to flow to our benefit and pleasure. Working to tear down racial barriers feels good. Nor should we forget that these monoamines (brain chemicals) are also good for our health. Friends of Critical Race Theory and of Civil Rights in general would do well to highlight these incentives. We'll consider these matters further and in more detail in the Conclusion. In preparation for that discussion, it is interesting to reflect on the comments of the father of modern Black Theology, a movement in Theology with close similarities to Critical Race Theory's contribution to the field of legal studies. Looking to the future, this famous theologian James Cone wrote:

> I think it is time ... to move beyond a mere reaction to white racism in America and begin to extend our vision of a new socially constructed humanity in the whole inhabited world... For humanity is whole and cannot be isolated into racial and national groups. (1999, p.46)

Let's consider next in closing how Critical Race Theory, enriched by Christian and Constitutional insights, can help us get there.

Conclusion

Can Critical Race Theory Change America for the Better? Constitutional and Faith Insights

How about it, reader? Is Critical Race Theory really not as American and wholesome as the Constitution and Christian faith? If we get to that stage we might begin to remove a lot of the nastiness among Americans that's been rising to the surface and not allowed real debate. In its realism about our present circumstances regarding race relations, its appreciation that white supremacy is still in place, have we not provided the data to support this at the end of the second chapter? This author certainly thinks he has. And as for cynicism about government that this seems to introduce, if we do not teach CRT cynicism in the schools in this way, then we need to purge from public education the cynicism both Christian and Constitutional ways of looking at life introduce. After all, if we ever refer to a Christian understanding of American government, we must add to it that Christians are people who believe our government is flawed (by sin). And Madison himself recognized that the American governmental system that he and his colleagues had created was flawed regarding the representation of all American economic interests. In that sense, it would never be fully representative of all the factions in America. On this matter, he wrote in No. 35 of *The Federalist Papers:*

> The idea of an actual representation of all classes of the people by persons of each class is altogether visionary... It is said to be necessary that all classes of citizens should have some of their own number in the representative body in order their feelings and interests may be the better understood and attended to. But we have seen that this will never happen under any arrangement that leaves the votes of the people free.

No such thing as a perfect government. What is wrong with letting our youth learn that hard truth? How is that bad for America? Could it not give incentive for working to make things better, to establish what Nelson Bell called "mechanisms to make life bearable in a society where blacks are a permanent subordinate class" (1992, in Crenshaw et al., p.307)? Along with other, more optimistic versions of American history rooted in The Declaration of Independence, Critical Race Theory has a rightful place in our schools and in our public square as a plausible analysis of American history and our present social realities.

Of course, a Constitutional critique of CRT could still be in order. In its effort to avoid formalism and objectivity in favor of sensitivity to outcomes of the court's judgments, it could be argued that this approach puts the judicial system in a position of determining what should be good laws (the job of the legislative branch), when in fact the task of the judiciary is to base its judgments on what laws are already laws. This is another example of how the critical, perspectival interpretative suppositions of CRT lead to distortions and chaos.

At least two responses might be made by CRT proponents to this critique. We could charge the judiciary with the task of evaluating the utility of laws, judgments, which would not affect the case's Constitutionality and the judgment rendered, but could function as advice to lawmakers. Or perhaps the courts could find in some cases that laws leading to bad outcomes for victims of discrimination are violations of the Constitution, and so on such grounds outcomes could have a legitimate role in the judicial discernment processes.

The other critique which could be raised about CRT (really intended as a friendly suggestion) would be to avoid charges of separatism by being more explicit about its compatibilities with Christian commitments and The Constitution. This could better position CRT for making an impact on American society as a whole. To be sure, some critics contend that Critical Race Theory, with its suspicions about liberal white motives, leads to a separatism. And as we have noted, the Critical Standpoint Epistemology of Critical Race Theory could preclude a real Black-white dialogue if it were allowed to stand (for it opens the door to believing that whites can never truly share Black concerns because they are not Black). Recall this Critical Epistemology is rooted in the reflections of Immanuel Kant who himself displayed racist points of view (see p.14, above). No such problems emerge if we read The Constitution and reality in Douglass' common-sense way, for then we can identify together what the document says and use it as well as our common moral principles (the natural law) to rule out race-neutral schools of interpretation. Besides, Neurobiological research, as we have indicated, allows for the possibility of this mode of interpretation.

Proponents of Critical Race Theory lose nothing by granting this point, as such an epistemology does not rule out the telling of unique Black stories or the role of Black culture (such as its music, art, and business contributions) to create interest and fresh insights in American society as a whole. Indeed, as CRT advocate John Galmore suggests (see pp.18-19, above), these elements of Black culture could function to overcome/critique the white supremacy that in the view of another CRT advocate Charles Lawrence (in Crenshaw et al., p.51) has diminished the possibility of the Black community forming effective majority coalitions. Intriguing, unique elements of Black culture may in principle just be a key ingredient to making the Constitutional system work more justly.

I do not want to close this book with proposed amendments to CRT, but with a celebration of what its insights bring to us all. The realism of Critical Race Theory reminds us of what is so helpful in our Constitutional system and deeply embedded in Christian convictions. Nothing will ever be perfect in the world or in American society. And none of us can change it alone. We have noted that cooperation is what makes human beings unique creatures. We have read of calls for collaboration and multiculturalism in CRT (albeit among minorities) from the likes of John Calmore (see p.25, above) as well as Richard Delagdo and Jean Stefancic in the name of CRT (pp.20ff.,83-84). The concepts of Intersectionality of oppression and Interest Convergence also presuppose at least cautious openness (at least when it is a coalition with whites) to building coalitions in the interests of the Black community.

We have observed that building coalitions, managing and disempowering factions, is how our Constitutional system operates. But there is no way to get rid of factions, and so the thing to do is to balance them in such a way that compromises lead to everyone's interests being protected (see 45ff, above). That takes coalitions and alliances among society's factions. Critical Race Theorists have reminded us, though, that minority group rights have been revocable by majority white aims (see pp.23-24, above). Thus, the most effective coalitions in Black interests will be those that endure over time. This insight is in the spirit of Martin Luther King, who in a work interestingly enough on Black Power, wrote:

> A true alliance is based upon some self-interest of each component group and a common interest into which they merge. For an alliance to have permanence and loyal commitment from its various elements, each of them must have a goal from which it benefits and none must have an outlook in basic conflict with its members. (June 1967, in 1986, p.309)

Interestingly enough, King's reflections also converge with CRT forefather Nelson Bell, who contended that further progress on racial issues might be possible "to the extent that the divergence of racial issues can be avoided or minimized." (1980, in Crenshaw et al., p.24) CRT authors have also provided insight on how to construct these coalitions. Like all in collective bargaining, negotiations and overtures must come from a position of strength, not weakness, helping the potential partner to see what such a coalition might offer him/her. It is at this point that stressing the uniqueness of Black culture, breaking with the integration model, could be of use in the early stage of coalition building. We have noted how CRT proponent John Calmore has contended that reliance on the Black cultural heritage might be an aid in social critique. In functioning as an oppositional movement it challenges the universality of white experience, Black culture can provide the kind of interesting alternatives which can capture the interest of the broader American population (see p.25-26, above). (CRT and its impact on the schools, the controversy this has touched off, is a good example.)

This is another reason why it is important for Black men and women to define themselves to have their own strong institutions. Such Black Power is not separatism, as critics of CRT suggest. It is simply a way of making sure that these African-American alternatives are not just unwitting "colored versions" of white agendas, that what is advocated for is truly good for Black folks. And the exercise of power in Black institutions and movements entails that the dialogue about forming coalitions emerges from positions of strength. White readers do well to remember that the next time they encounter or think about Black fraternities, Black professional organizations and interest groups, or Black businesses and schools. They are not about segregation and separating from whites. In fact, in celebrating Black culture and experience, these organizations/ movements make meaningful partnerships with others more likely.

Let's return to the realism about human nature and what can be accomplished in a society taught by Critical Race Theory, Christian faith, and The Constitution. This realism can be a resource in making change. We have already noted that the great American Social Ethicist Reinhold Niebuhr was an influence on M. L. King's realism (see p.66, above). Niebuhr believed that such Realism led to humility, and such humility, he claimed, can make us a lot easier to deal with and more cooperative. On this subject he wrote:

> One of the great resources of this faith for social achievement is the sense of humility which must result from the recognition of our common sinfulness... To subject human righteousness to the righteousness of God is to realize the imperfection of all our perfections, the taint of interest in all our virtues, and the natural limitations of our ideals. Men who are thus prompted to humility may differ in their ideals; but they will know themselves in the fact that they must differ... (1991, pp.132-133)

Elsewhere, Niebuhr elaborates further on this point. Humility makes people realize that their "best" ideas are provisional, and that makes them more tolerant of the opponent:

> We make such provisional judgments, but all these provisional judgments stand ultimately under the truth of the parable of the wheat and the tares. "Let both grow together until the harvest." (1974, p.58)

> Thus human history is a mixture of wheat and tares. We must make provisional distinctions, but we must know that there are no final

distinctions... But he [humanity] must also remember that no matter how high his creativity may rise, he is himself involved in the flow of time, and he becomes evil at the precise point where he pretends not to be, when he pretends that his wisdom is not finite but infinite, and his virtue is not ambiguous but unambiguous. (*Ibid.*, p.59)

If my wisdom is finite, then the opponent is not totally evil. He/She might teach me something I do not know. And if I do not realize the finiteness of my judgments about how good a law and the status quo in America are, my selfishness may be skewing that judgment. It may be that the law or status quo seems so good, because it is only good and just for me. That is how and why white supremacy looks so good for white folks. CRT is proclaiming nothing more than that point. Is that such a bad lesson to teach?

But how about the hopelessness or cynicism associated with realism sometimes? It is this sense of Racial Realism that so infuriates CRT critics, as it suggests that America is a lost cause, for as Nelson Bell claimed "Black people will never gain full equality in this country," that they "must acknowledge the permanence of ... subordinate status." (1992, p.306). He further adds to this (p.308):

While implementing Racial realism we must simultaneously acknowledge that our actions are not likely to lead to transcendent change and, despiteour best efforts, may be of more help to the system we despise than to the victims of the system we are trying to help.

We don't want this pessimism taught in our schools and in society the critics say. Perhaps we must also reflect on whether such a critique of the Civil Rights heritage leads to Black pessimism or hopelessness. What happens then to the King Dream and the Biological drive in homo sapiens towards cooperation which we have noted?

I have been asking this question about how to assess Racial Realism among friends in the Black (theological) community. There seems to be a consensus from my informal poll. There is a sad endorsement of the reality that perhaps we may never achieve real justice. But my contacts are not willing to surrender the ideals of the Civil Rights Movement, even though they concede that this ideal will never be fully achieved. I heard references to the need for dreams. Of course, we know of Dr. King's famous dream in his Washington speech, and Abolitionist Harriet Tubman once spoke of how having dreams can change the world, as she claimed that "Every great dream begins with a dreamer. Always remember, you have within you the strength, the patience, and the passion to reach for the stars to change the world." The hope of equality, despite the racial and political realities, might be deemed a way of strengthening the patience of Black men and women still seeking to change the world.

African-American poet and key contributor to the Harlem Renaissance Langston Hughes wrote," Hold Fast To Your Dreams, For When Dreams Die, Life Is A Broken-Winged Bird That Cannot Fly." Without dreams, nothing new really happens. Even though we know better, that the King Dream and the promises of The Declaration of Independence can never be fully realized, they give us what Barak Obama called "The Audacity of Hope" for something better. We have already noted that CRT proponent Charles Lawrence (see p.25, above) contends that Black radicalism entails the gift to dream.

These images about the need for dreams could be seen as compatible with CRT thinking. Derrick Bell claimed that even if transcendent change on racial matters is not likely, this realization need not lead to passivity. He writes in "Racial Realism" (p.308):

> Nevertheless, our realization, and the dedication based on that realization, can lead to policy positions and campaigns that are less likely to worsen conditions for those we are trying to help and more likely to those in power that there are imaginative, unabashed risk-takers who refuse to be trammeled upon... Continued struggle can bring about unexpected benefits and gains that in themselves justify continued endeavor. The fight itself has meaning and should give us hope for the future.

The continued realistic activism to attack white dominance in American society for which CRT opts can still make things better in America, "even if it ain't the ideal." Of course, that's all The Constitution and Christianity say is possible. This is the way in which the critique of present American structures and the nation's racist past should be understood – part of the effort to develop a community that at least makes it less likely that the community will get worse. Referring to the vision of Martin Luther King, Jr. Anthony Cook (p.101) claimed:

> In conclusion, I believe the postmodern preoccupation with deconstruction is but a precursor to serious reflection on how we should live in community... In this regard, our assessment of the problems can be no better than the lenses through which we examine these problems... The process must be deliberative, participatory, and respectful of difference and diversity.

All the critique of America launched by CRT aims at enhancing dialogue and community (in the best traditions of The Constitution).

Another theme that emerged from my informal poll and conversations in the Black community about the viability of the concept of Racial Realism was drawn from Scientific insights (esp. those of Physics and Einstein's findings). One Black scientist turned theologian, Everett Flanigan, suggested that while such realism is correct, we need the King Dream and the ideals of the Constitution to provide the **energy** (the basis of all that exists) it takes to activate our community engagement.

Several of my conversation partners, convinced that Racial Realism makes sense opted for thinking about community work and writing to take the form of Prophecy – a role long played by the Black community and the Black church (Evans; C. West:97-108). These commitments seem in line with some CRT thinking. For prophecy is a way of saying "no" to the establishment, pointing to the eschatological dream of freedom, peace, and justice. And Derrick Bell described Racial Realism (in his article with that title, p.309) in a manner similar to this, when he wrote:

> We must realize, as our slave forebears did, that the struggle for freedom is, at bottom, a manifestation of our humanity which survives and grows stronger through resistance to oppression, even if that oppression is never overcome.

It seems that CRT teaches us to take the King Dream of the Beloved Community as an alternative vision of a community which can survive and even grow stronger as we continue to struggle against racism. CRT advocate Anthony Cook (p.101) takes a similar position on the King Dream and the ideals of the Civil Right Movement when he claims that such ideals can be "a stone of hope" hewn from the mountain of racial despair. Perhaps we could begin to construe all the references to freedom and equality in The Constitution in this light.

Another image for understanding the CRT agenda of realism that I find personally moving is to construe the reality of Black (and white) anti-racist fighters as rebels, in the sense that Albert Camus used the image. For Camus (pp.13-14) a rebel is:

> A man who says no, but whose refusal does not imply a renunciation. He is also a man who says yes from the moment he makes his first gesture of rebellion... In a certain way, he confronts an order of things which oppress him with an insistence on a kind of right not to be oppressed beyond the limit that he can tolerate...

In every act of rebellion, the rebel simultaneously experiences a feeling of revulsion at the infringement of his rights and a complete and spontaneous loyalty to certain aspects of himself.

And yet rebellion is not purely negative for Camus (pp.304-305), but like Bell and Cook it glimpses something positive in the human spirit as its end. He adds:

Rebellion proves in this way that it is the very movement of life... At the end of this tunnel of darkness, however, there is inevitably a light which we already divine and for which we only have to fight to ensure its coming.

You might be "woke" when you are fighting Anti-Racism, but how about thinking of this task and the CRT mission as rebellion (in Camus' sense of the term). It is rebellion against the chaos, meaninglessness, and injustice of modern American life. It is a ways of asserting our humanity, and this is precisely how CRT forefather Derrick Bell (1992, p.308) understood the struggle against racism. But as Anthony Cook, speaking from a CRT perspective reminds us, this rebellion is about action, not just thought, has a positive dimension. In his article, "Beyond Critical Legal Studies" (p.101) he wrote:

Let us not fall victim to the paralysis of neural analysis. Instead, we must meet and talk together, appreciating our respective histories and experiences of alienation and oppression. We must talk specifically about the kind of community we would fashion and how the rules, laws, and rituals defining the role we adopt can be mutually empowering and facilitative of a community of equals. We must talk specifically about how we should organize, protest, agitate, and struggle to achieve our objective, realizing that we are perennially engaged in a dialectic in which the program shapes our practices, which in turn refine and redefine our program.

Closing Thoughts and Possible Practices

It is evident that Critical Race Theory shares a lot of common commitments with The Constitution and Christian faith, is it not? And we have established that CRT is not excluding dialogue with other communities, not solely focused on a Black point of view in its insistence that a self-defined Black point of view needs to take the lead in order to ensure that that viewpoint is not co-opted and redefined by white supremacy. It is not advocating a separatism which countermands the findings of Biology about how homo sapiens are more likely to enjoy Evolutionary advantages when we cooperate (see pp.68ff., above).

Indeed, Evolutionary Biology seems to countenance and encourage the formation of local autonomous groups formed on the basis of common ethnicities, skills, and agendas without a larger corpus. Nobel Prize-winning Economist Elinor Ostrom (see D. Wilson, pp.116ff.) has developed eight core principles for institutions based on the Theory of Evolution. All these principles facilitate cooperation, but one of them posits the formation of such local autonomous groups which then contribute to the broader institution. There you have it: Biology teaches us that special Black-interest groups in larger bodies contribute to cooperation. Would that not be an important Biological as well as Social Studies learning for children in our schools?

But it would not be in the spirit of CRT, Cook seems to claim, if we just stopped our analysis of Critical Race Theory with these conceptual points about possible CRT convergences of viewpoints with these and other models. On the other hand, however, it also does not seem appropriate for me, especially not as a Norwegian American, to describe what the new community for which CRT is advocating would look like.

At this point, I could simply cite the recommendations I have co-authored with a rising Black Civil Rights leader, James Woodall, in a book titled *Wired For Racism? How Evolution and Faith Move Us to Challenge Racial Idolatry*. You might want to consider the book yourself to get a more detailed picture of how we see a way out of white supremacy and racial idolatry. The solutions we offer are very much in the spirit of CRT. With the theorists considered in this book, we highlight that race is not a Biological distinction, but a cultural one, that racism is more a structural and institutional matter (we also argue that our brains are tilted in that direction unless carefully monitored) than a personal one, and that racism (fighting what we call racial idolatry) needs to be a focus in our examination of American society and its institutions. OK, let's take a look at how Critical Race Theory, in dialogue with The Constitution and an Augustinian Christian viewpoint might address today's issues and, on the basis of these insights, provide insights into what alternatives to the present racist structures/practices might look like.

Policing:

The racial disparities in arrests (see pp.31-32, above) based as a result of prevailing Comp Stats methods of police deployment need to be challenged, with more implementation of alternatives such as Community Policing.

Disparities in Judicial Sentencing:

The United States Sentencing Commission found in its 2017 report titled "Demographic Differences in Sentencing" that Black males were given sentences at a rate of 19.1% longer than white males for the same crime. I have not yet encountered CRT proposals for addressing this disparity. Of course, we know that some sentences are harsher for crimes more characteristic in Black neighborhoods (crack use rather than powder cocaine). But that can be remedied with legislation, which as CRT urges, is always formulated and informed by examining the impact of a law on Black communities. But what to do about different sentences for the same crime? Mandatory sentencing clearly is not the answer, as that fails to take into account the special challenges Black men and women face (as ineffective and racist as "Color-Blindness" in law). Requiring prospective and retroactive racial impact statements for all criminal statutes would certainly be relevant to legislation and might have some impact on disparate Black-white sentencing. Likewise, taking a hard look at the racial imbalance in the prison system might also contribute to more justice in sentencing. A proposal by CRT proponent Dorothy Roberts (1991, in Critical Legal Studies et al., pp.404-405) to expand the right of privacy to drug prosecutions and also to expand this right to the government's duty to protect the individual's personhood and offer drug treatment may have promise. The Constitutional and Christian appeal to the natural law (to strictures against theft and not doing the neighbor harm, especially recalling the special Christian and Constitutional references to aiding the poor) might also function as arguments to further the CRT agenda on this matter. But perhaps the problem of unequal sentencing based on race relates to the next area of racial abuse we consider. Maybe the best we can do is to try to sensitize the judiciary to their innate racial biases.

Media and Images in Pop Culture:

Negative media and social images of people of color are well known. Positive representation through mass media, including in Hollywood and Broadway along with more balance in the reporting of news is crucial to this process. Nor should we forget recent research demonstrating how many algorithms of our search engines reinforce racism (Noble). With more positive Black images embedded in pop culture, the biased-inclined judges or the nervous cop, might be less inclined to hand down the longer sentence or pull the trigger on Brothers and Sisters.

It may be that leveling the economic playing field is the right formula for bringing about this cultural shift. Perhaps enabling more African-American ownership in the movie and television business is all it would take. Another promising trend is an appreciation of the fact that a growing market of non-whites will prod media moguls to appeal to this growing market. Since the market has not yet achieved this, the reflections of CRT proponents Patricia Williams, "Metro Broadcasting Inc v. FCC Regrouping in Singular Times" (in Crenshaw et al, pp.191ff.) are most relevant. Regarding how the Supreme

Court's decision as a result of the lawsuit named in the just cited article, she contends it is evident that active steps must be taken to ensure that broadcast diversification has implications for ownership. Minority set-asides and Affirmative Action are the way to go in resolving these issues. As Williams (p.199) writes:

> Equal opportunity is not only about assuming the circumstances of hypothetically indistinguishable individuals; it is also about accommodating the living, shifting fortunes of those who are very differently situated.

These reflections seem helpful in addressing the next range of issues.

Economics and Jobs:

We previously noted the wage gap between Black and white in America (see p.28, above). All sorts of factors account for this, not least of all including the difficulties African Americans have in getting jobs and loans (pp.28,30, above) to start their businesses due to biases built into the system. On this topic too, Affirmative Action seems the way to go. Anti-discrimination laws are not enough. For without positive action on behalf of minorities, anti-discrimination laws leave in place the racist economic and systemic dynamics still in place (Freeman, in Crenshaw et al., esp. pp.31-32). To be sure, there may be some resemblance at this point to Socialism (though not necessarily Marxism). And CRT is not alone in advocating for something like these policies. The Constitution's Founders did so, we have noted, and a special concern for the poor is a Christian value (see Chapters 3 and 4). If Critical Race Theory is too radical, so are all the theologians and Founders we have cited.

CRT proponents like Mari Matsuda (in Crenshaw et al., pp.72-73.) posit the need for reparations to compensate for injustices, and would have those entitled to relief to be determined by groups "at the bottom." But this provocative proposal seems to overlook the Constitutional supposition that all factions are self-interested, and so perhaps inclined to take unfair advantage of certain systems. Perhaps an alternative to this, informed by the realism about the human nature of CRT, the Constitution, and the Christian faith, would be to provide reparations in the amount claimants could demonstrate that jobs (or promotions) were not held/offered or loans not extended due to race would have increased their wealth (calculating not just for salaries and profits, but also estimated savings over the period of damage), and then to be recompensed in that amount. Another option has been proposed by Economists William Darity and A. Kirsten Mullen in their book *From Here to Equality: Reparations for Black Americans in the Twenty-First Century* (esp. pp.2,4,31). They espouse paying every African American who can demonstrate ancestry in slavery the equivalent (allowing for inflation and family investments of that wealth since 1865) of the amount of the promised 40 acres and a mule on which the US never delivered as compensation for services as slaves.

All of Matsuda's concerns that reparations offer Constitutional affirmations of the personhood of victims, their liberty, and resources for the future can be offered in the preceding and my alternative proposals. (It might also have the virtue of having a better chance of getting through Congress someday.) But in any case, whether or not this alternative is more readily implemented, CRT provides interesting options.

Another way of addressing the economic disparities caused by racism and the economic disparities in general might be to return to a model proposed in the Civil Rights era by Martin Luther King, Jr. in his last book, *Where Do We God from Here: Chaos or Community?* (in 1986, p.616) – the guaranteed income "pegged to the median income of society, not at the lowest levels." More recently, both Andrew Yang, during his 2020 Presidential campaign and Mark Zuckerberg in his 2017 Harvard commencement speech, offered this fertile proposal.

Housing:

The practices of red-lining housing in Black neighborhoods is well known (pp.29-30, above). Houses or apartments in a Black neighborhood comparable to ones in a predominantly white neighborhood will most always be worth less than the house on the other side of town. And loans for mortgages are easier to obtain by whites than they are for Blacks. Once again, reparations seem to be the way to go (we have noted in previous chapters that both The Constitution's Founders and Christian faith allow for the possibility). Aggrieved families would be entitled to reparations in the amount of the difference that lower property values were a function of the location of their home in a Black neighborhood and also in the case of rejections of mortgages due to race to the amount of equity they could have accumulated over their lifetimes owning that house. For all of these ways of looking at life, property is always to be subordinated to individual well-being.

Health Care:

We have already noted the racial gap in health care and its outcomes (p.31, above). A major, but by no means the only factor accounting for this is access to free healthcare.   The Affordable Care Act of the Obama administration was a step in the right direction. But universal healthcare coverage after the fashion of the Western European social democracies seems the way to go. The medical and political communities also need to come to terms with research indicating that shorter Black life expectancy relates to the stresses of racism, for such stress wears out cells leading to premature aging (Geronimus et al; 199-234). Realizing the CRT (and its allies') agenda can be good for Black health.

Environment:

Most people have heard of the contaminated water in Grand Rapids, Michigan and Jackson, Mississippi. A 2021 study funded by the Environmental Protection Agency found a 15% difference between Blacks and whites regarding exposure to pollution. Obviously, remedying this is a matter of economics and politics, either employing the economic pressures against racism already noted, or deploying CRT principles of requiring all laws and zoning ordinances to consider prospective and retroactive racial impact statements.

Voting and Gerrymandering:

We have already considered practices of racism (see p.32, above) implemented through the gerrymandering of Black voters in Congressional and State House Districts in ways that as much as possible make them minority voices along with the voting restrictions on the poor and the previously incarcerated. Obviously, we need legislation to stop these practices. Again, implementing CRT principles requiring all laws to consider prospective and retroactive racial impact statements could make a real contribution here. We can also appeal to comments by James Madison who noted:

> The right of suffrage is a fundamental Article in Republican Constitutions. The regulation of it is, at the same time, a task of peculiar delicacy. Allow the right [to vote] exclusively to property [owners], and the rights of persons may be oppressed...

As we have noted, the compromise in The Constitution itself, leaving the issue of who could vote seemed effectively to allow **all** citizens the vote given the political realities of the States at that time, and the document's critical position toward slavery eventually enabled the amendments opening doors to the votes of Blacks and all women.

One other action with CRT blessing that we would do well to consider is getting money out of politics. The present system favors the rich and the influence on politicians (who need big bucks for the exorbitant campaign expenses) that money can buy. Given the wealth deficit in the Black community, like most things in America, the system favors white supremacy. And since such election dynamics will likely land candidates in office who are indebted to these white interests, the next rounds of legislation will be favoring the rich white classes.

A first step in ending this cycle might be legislation to mandate cutting campaign costs. Another possibility would be public financing of elections. In both cases, this would undercut the influence of corporate lobbyists so that the poor and working classes, along with the Black voice might matter more.

Education:

By now, most every reader will have heard about all controversy over teaching Black Lives Matter in the schools, and we also need to come to terms with the data previously cited about how racism continues to plague our public schools (see pp.30-31, above). Derrick Bell (1980, in Crenshaw et al., p.20) raised the question at the outset of the development of Critical Race Theory about whether integration had been good for the Black community, and it is as clear as when he raised the issue that most Black children continue to "attend public schools that are both racially isolated and inferior." White supremacy is still in place even after Brown v. Board of Education. And the dominance of a white supremacy curriculum (or at least the desire to maintain it) is evidenced in the protests against Critical Race Theory by school boards and legislatures sweeping across the nation.

CRT is already in some of the schools, if not directly, at least indirectly, in its challenges to their white supremacy curriculum and the administrative style of many school districts, which is classist (most money going to the school districts or schools within a district with the highest tax base). In our book, *Wired For Racism?*, James Woodall and I provided a detailed analysis of the classism (and so racism) of the public school system and what to do about it. (Yes, even the way we teach kids in poverty, a disproportionate number of these children being Black, is classist, and so racist.) In this context, suffice it to note CRT commitments to evaluating all laws and institutions in relation to their prospective and retroactive racial impact. It just seems fair, does it not, to have a commitment to making things right in our schools for a group of people who have suffered oppression at the hands of American institutions for more than 400 years? Is it really so radical or Communist? Just seems fair, Christian, even Constitutional.

Same goes with the curricular issues, which are receiving so much media attention. For a group of people, whose history and contributions are so little known (few whites know that 4% of Washington's Revolutionary Army was Black, that a Black man, Garrett Morgan, invented the traffic light, or about the Black millionaires of the nineteenth century), don't we now need to make Americans learn about these gaps in our education? You hear complaints about Black Studies departments in colleges, but nobody I know has ever critiqued the existence of the Dutch Department at Calvin University or the Norwegian Department of St. Olaf College!

Of course the critique in our schools of the white supremacist character of American institutions is another (perhaps the primary) concern. Let's wrap things up with a consideration of that matter.

Is Critical Race Theory of Any Use to America?

A lot of conservatives do not want all the negativity about America CRT seems to bring. In their view, it is un-American, even demeaning the virtues of the Civil Rights heritage. It unduly lays guilt on whites and undermines Black initiative by making them victims. It's so un-Constitutional and un-Christian. I think we have refuted these charges. The only links to Marxism are that some CRT modes of interpretation are indebted to Marxist thinkers. But that surfaces only in CRT criticism of belief that texts have a descriptive meaning apart from the context of their creation and their author's intention. As we have seen, that idea is not new to academics since the Enlightenment. For Kant's belief that all truth is relative to the subject's point of view and now we call it DeConstruction or PostModernism (see the discussion on p. 14, above) has saturated most of our colleges and even the curriculum of our public schools (Bloom, pp.148-149). Indeed, the Educational Theory proposed in the 1970s by Brazilian Marxist scholar Paulo Freire in his *Pedagogy of the Oppressed* shares the CRT, DeConstructionist critique of the possibility of establishing or teaching common facts. And his book on Education is reportedly one of the most frequently required texts used in teacher college courses in the US (see Butcher, pp.61-62). But the public does not seem all in arms about these developments.

Confession: I have concerns about the relativism this way of interpreting texts and reality leads to. I prefer the approach of Frederick Douglass, to believe that with hard work and research we can arrive at a text's meaning apart from our perspective or the text's original context, that sometimes this meaning is not what the writer had in mind. It's the way scientists operate (see my book *Ever Hear of Feuerbach?*, esp. pp.93-98,100-101). This interpretive approach could help CRT by allowing it to appeal like Douglass to Constitutional themes which support the liberation agenda, with less concern about illicit conservative interpreters claiming their perspective is a valid one. Science operates with these suppositions (that some realities can be descriptively analyzed regardless of one's orientation), and so why not law? But just the same, with the exception of Benedict XVI in one of his homilies, and even Catholic schools have not listened to him, the media and the pundits do not seem to bent out of shape by relativist suppositions in our schools and colleges, so why pick on Critical Race Theory?

If you do not like the apparent pessimism of CRT and its condemnation of racism, better purge The Constitution and references to historic Christian teaching, because they are downright pessimistic. Teach the Constitution and kids will learn they are all selfish (self-interested). And in the Church, they will even learn they are all sinners. In those settings, they will even learn that as long as they live, those realities cannot be overcome. Why these worldviews are outrageous (at least as outrageous as CRT)!

Does all this lead to defeatism and passivity for African Americans, knowing that full justice can never be achieved and that you have been victimized? From this realist perspective The Constitution has encouraged efforts to make America better (through the Amendment process) and the Church has taught its member to be prophetic and "called out" from (in rebellion against) the ways of the world, even to care for the poor. (We've seen that theme of redistribution of wealth implied in the Constitution.) Does such realism about what we can accomplish necessarily lead to passivity? Think of all the agenda's for justice and uplift CRT. It is as Derrick Bell (1992, p.308) wrote:

> I am convinced that there is something real out there in America for black people...we must maintain the struggle against racism, else the erosion of black rights will become even worse than it is now.

I think I hear in this racial realism echoes of Barak Obama's "audacity of hope." A worldview like this that makes rights better for Black folks, gives strategies for coping and making things better, helps us all know the score can't be all bad for America. Seems like it could improve things. And like I've shown, if you don't want to expose others to its critiques and realism, its warnings about the majority being prone to take advantage of minorities, better not teach The Constitution or expose our young to the Christian faith either.

In our book *Wired For Racism?*, James Woodall and I have shown that whatever can help tear down white supremacy and get us better working together in realistic, power-sharing cooperative ways, is good for human evolution (because Evolution instructs us that we are at our best as humans when we are cooperating). And when we cooperate, work together for equal rights, our brains reward us with the secretion of pleasurable brain chemicals. Fighting racism feels good when you do it with others. So what is all the fuss about over Critical Race Theory? Maybe the real answer is, after all, that it's about not wanting to be critical of the racism we find in America and its institutions.

Bibliography

Adams, John. Letter. 1775.

_____ The *Works of John Adams, Second President of the United States.* Edited by Charles Adams. Boston: Charles Little & James Brown, 1850-1856.

AliSafaat, Muchammad and Istiqomah, Milda. "Critical Legal Studies [CLS]: An Alternative for Critical Legal Thinking in Indonesia," *Journal Kajian Ilmu Hukurn dan Syaria* 7, No.1 [2022]:11; "Critical Legal Studies," in Encyclopedia.com)

Ansell, Amy. "Critical Race Theory, in Richard Schaeffer, ed., *Encyclopedia of Race, Ethnicity, and Society*, Vol.1. Melbourne, Aus.: Sage Publications, 2008, pp.344-346.

Athanasius. *The Incarnation of the Word of God.* 318.

Augustine. *City of God.* 413-426.

_____ *Confessions.* 399.

_____ *On Marriage and Concupiscence.* 418/420.

_____ *Ten Homilies On The First Epistle of John.* ca.417.

_____ *To Simplician.* 396/398.

_____ *On the Spirit and the Letter.* 412.

Banks, JoAnne. "Talk that Talk: Storytelling and Analysis Rooted in African American Oral Tradition." *Qualitative Health Research.* 2002: 410ff.

Barth, Karl. *Church Dogmatics.* Edited by G. W. Bromiley and T. F. Torrance. 4 vols. Edinburgh: T.and T. Clark, 1936-1962.

Baucham, Voddie. *Fault Lines: The Social Justice Movement and Evangelicalism's Looming Catastrophe.* Washington: Salem Boks, 2021.

Bell, Derrick. "Brown v. Board of Education and the Interest Convergence Dilemma," *Harvard Law Review*, 1980: 518-533.

_____ *Confronting Authority: Reflections of an Ardent Protestor.* Boston, Beacon, 1994.

_____. *Race, Racism, and American Law.* New York: Aspen, 2004.

_____. "Racial Realism," *Connectical Law Review* 24 [2], 1992: 364ff.

_____. "Serving Two Masters: Integration Ideals and Client Interests in School Desegregation Litigation," *Yale Law Journal* 1976: 470-516.

Benedict XVI. Homily for the Mass *Pro Eligendo Romano Pontifice.* April, 2005.

Berkeley, George. *A Treatise concerning the Principles of Human Knowledge.* 1710.

Bloom, Allan. *The Closing of the American Mind.* New York: Simon & Schuster, 1987.

Bonilla-Silva, Eduardo. *Racism Without Racists: Color-Blind Racism and the Persistence of Racial Inequality in America.* Lanham, MD: Rowman & Littlefield, 2017.

Butcher, Jonathan. *Splintered: Critical Race Theory and the Progressive War on Truth.* New York and Nashville, TN: Post Hill Press, 2022.

Butterfield, L. H. *John Witherspoon Comes to America.* Princeton, NJ: Princeton University Press, 1953.

Calvin, John. *Institutes of the Christian Religion.* 1536/1541.

Camus, Albert. *The Rebel.* Translated by Anthony Bower. New York: Vintage Books, 1956.

Clement of Alexandria. *The Instructor.* n.d.

Clement of Rome. Epistle To the Corinthians. 96.

Commodianus. *The Instructions.* ca240 – ca250.

Cone, James. "Black Theology in American Religion." *Journal of American Academy of Religion* LIII, No.4 [December 1985]: 755-772.

_____ *Risks of Faith.* Boston: Beacon Press, 1999.

Cook, Anthony. "Beyond Critical Legal Studies: The Reconstructive theology of Dr. Martin Luther King, Jr." *Harvard Law Review.* 1991.

Crenshaw, Kimberlé. "Mapping the Margins: Interesectionality, Identity, Politics, and Violence Against Women of Color." *Stanford Law Review* 43, No.6 (July, 1991): 1241-1299.

_____. "Op Ed: King was a critical race theorist before there was a name for it." *Los Angeles Times,* Jan. 17 2022.

_____. "Race, Reform, Retrenchment: Transformation and Legitimation in Antidiscrimination Law," *Harvard Law Review* 1331 (1988).

_____. *Theory: The Key Writings That Formed the Movement.* New York: The New Press, 1995.

"Critical Legal Studies Movement." *The Bridge* [n.d.], https://cyber.harvard.edu/bridge/CriticalTheory/critical2.htm

Curry, Oliver S., Mullins, Daniel, and Whitehouse, Harvey. "It is Good To Cooperate?, *Cultural Anthropology,* 2019).

Cyprian of Carthage. *Epistles.* n.d.

Dalton, Harlon. The Clouded Prism: Minority Critique of the Critical Legal Studies Movement," *Harvard Civil Rights – Civil Liberties Law Review* 22, Issue 2 [Spring, 1987]:436-439.

Darity, William and Mullen, A. Kirsten. *From Here to Equality: Reparations for Black Americans in the Twenty-First Century.* Chapel Hill, NC: University of North Carolina Press, 2020.

Dawkins, Richard. *The Selfish Gene.* London: Oxford University Press, 1976.

Delgado, Richard and Stefancic, Jean. *Critical Race Theory: An Introduction.* 3rd ed.; New York: New York University Press, 2017.

Derrida, Jacques. *Grammatology.* Translated by Gayatri Spivak. Baltimore and London: Johns Hopkins University Press, 1976.

Douglas, Kelly B. *Stand Your Ground: Black Bodies and the Justice of God,* Maryknoll, NY: Orbis, 2015.

Douglass, Frederick. "Speech before the Scottish Anti-Slavery Society." 1860.

Dunn, John. "The Politics of Locke in England and America in the Eighteenth Century," *John Locke: Problems and Perspectives.* Edited by J. W. Yolton. London: Cambridge University Press, 1969

Einstein, Albert. Letter, February 12, 1950.

Ellingsen, Mark. *Ever Hear of Feuerbach? That's Why American and European Christianity Are in Such a Funk!* Eugene, OR: Cascade, 2020.

_____. and Woodall, James. *Wired For Racism? How Evolution and Faith Move Us to Challenge Racial Idolatry.* Hyde Park, NY: New City Press, 2022.

Evans, James. "The Prophetic Role of the African American Churches in the 21st Century." *Reflections*, 2006.

Farber, Daniel and Sherry, Suzanna. *Beyond All Reason: The Radical Assault on Truth in American Law.* London: Oxford University Press, 1997.

Fletcher, Jeannine Hill. *The Sin of White Supremacy: Christianity, Racism, and Religious Diversity in America.* Mayknoll, NY: Orbis Books, 2017.

Ford, Richard. "The Boundaries of Race: Political Geography and Legal Analysis." *Harvard Law Review* 107, No.8 (June, 1994).

Fortin, Jacey. "Critical race Theory: A Brief History." *New York Times.* November 8. 2021.

Foucault, Michel and Chomski, Noam. *Human Nture: Justice Versus Power.* Chicago: Souvenir Press, 2011.

Franklin, Benjamin. Letter to Robert Morris. 1783.

_____. *Proposals Relating to the Education of Youth in Pennsylvania.* 1740.

_____. *Writings.* New York: The Library of America, n.d.

Freeman, Alan. "Legitimizing Racial Discrimination through Antidiscriminational Law: A Critical Review of Supreme Court Doctrine." *Minnesota Law Review* 1978: 804ff.

Frei, Hans. *The Eclipse of Biblical Narrative.* New Haven, CT: Yale University Press, 1974.

Freire, Paulo. *Pedagogy of the Oppressed.* 30th Anniversary Edition. New York: Continuum, 2005.

Gaddis, Michael. "Discrimination in the Credential Society: An Audit Study of Race and College Selectivity in the Labor Market." *Social Forces* 93, No.4 [June 2015]: 1451-1479.

Geronimus, Arline et al. "Race/Ethnicity, Poverty, Urban Stressors, and Telomere Length in a Detroit Community-Based Sample." *Journal of Health and Social Behavior* 56 [June 2015]: 199-234.

Gotanda, Neil. "A Critique of 'Our Constitution Is Color-Blind," *Stanford Law Review*, 1991: 1.

Gramsci, Antonio. "Long March through the Institutions." *Conservapedia* (n.d), at https://www.conservapedia.com/Long_march_through_the_institutions.

_____ . *Selections From the Prison Notebooks.* New York: International Publishers, 1971.

Greene, Linda. "Race in the Twenty-First Century: Equality Through Law." *Tulane Law Review* 64, No.6 (1990).

Hamilton, Alexander. *The Framer Refuted*, 1775.

Harari, Yuval. *Sapiens: A Brief History of Humankind.* London: Harvill Secker, 2014.

Harris, Cherryl. "Whiteness as Property," *Harvard Law Review*, 1993.

Hoffman, Kelly et al, "Racial Bias in Pain Assessment and Treatment Recommendations, and False Beliefs About Biological Differences Between Blacks and Whites," *Proceedings of the National Academy of Sciences*, 2016: 4296-4300.

Holmes, Oliver Wendell. The Path of the Law," *Harvard Law Review* 459 [1897]

Horkheimer, Max. "Traditional and Critical Theory" and "The Present Situation of Social Philosophy and the Tasks of an Institute for Social Research," in *Between Philosophy and Social Science: Selected Early Writings*. Translated by John Torpey. Cambridge, MA: MIT Press 1993.

Hume, David. *An inquiry concerning Human Understanding*. 1748.

Hutcheson, Francis. *An Essay on the Nature and Conduct of the Passions and Affections with Illustrations on the Moral Sense*. 1742. 3rd edition; Gainesville, FL: Scholars' Facsimiles & Reprints, 1969.

_____. *An Inquiry into the Original of our Ideas of Beauty and Virtue*. 1725. New York: Garland, 1971.

Irenaeus. *Against Heresies*. ca180.

Jefferson, Thomas. Letter to Dr. Walter Jones. January 2, 1814.

_____. Letter to James Madison, 1785.

_____. Letter to Will Green Munford. 1799.

_____. Letter to Dugald Stewart, 1824.

_____. Letter to Robert Skipworth with a List of Books. 1771.

_____. "Notes On the State of Virginia." 1782.

_____. *Writings*. New York: Library Classics, 1984.

Jennings, Willie. *After Whiteness: A Education in Belonging*. Grand Rapids, MI: Wm. B. Eerdmans, 2020.

Jensen, Merrill, ed. *Documentary History of the Ratification of the Constitution*. Madison, WI: State Historical Society of Wisconsin, 1976ff.

John Paul II. *Redemptor Hominis*. 1979.

Johnson, Marcus. "The Republican Push to Ban Critical race Theory Reveals an Ugly Truth." *Newsweek*. May 5, 2021, https://www.newsweek.com/republican-push-ban-critical-race-theology-reveals-uglytruth-opinion-1588684.

Kaminsky, Thomas et al, eds. *Documentary History of the Ratification of the Constitution*, Vol.2. Madison, WI: State Hisorical Society of Wisconsin, 7.

Kant, Immanuel. *Critique of Pure Reason* (1787). Translated by Norman Kemp Smith. Toronto: Macmillan, 1929.

_____. *Zum ewigen Frieden: Ein philosophischer Entwurf*. Konigsberg: F. Nicolovius, 1795.

_____. *Prolegomena zu einer jeden künftigen Metaphysik*. Riga: Johnann Friedrich Hartknoch, 1764.

_____. *Von Den verscheidene Rassen der Menschen*. 1775.

Kendi, Ibram. *Summary: How To Be an Antiracist*. Xinbei, Taiwan: Knowledge Tree, 2020.

Kennedy, Duncan. "A Cultural Pluralist Case for Affirmative Action in Legal Academia," *Duke Law Journal* [1990]: 705-757.

_____. and Klare, Karl E. "A Bibliography of Critical Legal Studies." *Yale Law Journal*. 1984: 461.

King, Martin Luther, Jr. "Address to the 131st annual meeting of the New York State Convention of Universalists (NYSCU)," *Empire State Universalist*, 1956.

_____. "APA Annual Convention Address. 1967.

_____. "Birth of a New Nation." 1957.

_____. "Black Power Defined," *New York Times Magazine*, June 11, 1967.

_____. "Pilgrimage To Nonviolence," *The Christian Century*. 1960.

_____. "Remaining Awake Through a Geat Revolution." 1968.

_____. *A Testament of Hope: Thre Essential Writings ofMartin Luther King, Jr.* Edited by James Washington. New York: Harper & Row, 1986.

_____. *Where Do We God From Here? Chaos Or Community?* New York: Harper and Row, 1967.

Ladson-Billings, Gloria. "Just What is Critical Race Theory and What's It Doing in a Nice Field Like Education?" *International Journal of Qualitative Studies in Education* 11, No.1 (January 1998): 7-24.

Lawrence, Charles. "The Word and the River: Pedagogy as Scholarship as Struggle." *California Law Review* 65, Issue 5 (1992).

_____. "The ID, the EGO, and Equal Protection: Reckoning With Unconscious Racism." *Stanford Law Review* (1987).

Ledesma, Maria and Caldéron, Delores. "Critical Race Theory in Education: A Review of Past Literature and a Look into the Future." *Qualitative Inquiry* 21, No.3 (March 2015).

Lee, Jayne Chong-Soon, "Navigating the Topology of Race," Stanford Law Review Vol.46, No.3 (Feb.1994): 747-780.

Linn, Susan. *Who's Raising the Kinds? Big Tech. Big Business, and the Lives of Children*. New York and London: The New Press, 2022.

Locke, John. *Second Treatise on Civil Government*. 1690.

_____. *The Reasonableness of Christianity*. 1731.

Lohmeier, Matthew. *Irresistible Revolution: Marxism's Goal of Conquest & the Unmaking of the American Military*. Self-published, 2021.

Lopez, Henry. *White By Law: The Legal Construction of Race*. New York: NYU Press, 2006.

Luther, Martin. *D. Martin Luthers Werke*. Kritische Gesamtausgabe (Weimarer Ausgabe). Weiamr: Hermann Böhlaus Nachfolger, 1883ff. (heareafter cited as WA).

_____. *Admonition To Peace*. 1525.

_____. *Disputation Against Scholastic Theology*. 1517.

_____. *The Large Catechism*. 1529.

_____. *Lectures On Genesis* 1535-1545.

_____. *Lectures on Romans*. 1515-1516.

Lutz, Donald S. *The Origins of American Constitutionalism*. Baton Rouge, LA: Louisiana State University Press, 1988.

Madison, James, Hamilton, Alexander, and Jay, John. *The Federalist Papers*. 1788.

_____. Letter to Thomas Jefferson. 1790, in *Papers*, Vol.16. New York: Putnam, 1910.

_____. Letter to James Madison, Sr. 1769

_____. *Notes Of the Debates in the Federal Convention of 1787*. New York and London: W. W. Norton, 1987.

_____. 'parties." 1792.

Malone, Dumas. *Jefferson and His Time, I: Jefferson the Virginian*, Boston and New York: Little, Brown and Company, 1948.

Marcuse, Herbert. *Essay On Liberation*. Boston: Beacon Press, 1969.

Matsuda, Mari. "Looking to the Bottom: Critical Legal Studies and Reparations." *Harvard Civil Rights – Civil Liberties Law Review* 323. 1987.

Maxwell, David. *Race in Post-Obama America*. Louisville, KY: Westminster John Knox Press, 2016.

Meckler, Laura and Dawsey. "Republicans Spurred by an Unlikely Figure, See Political Promise In Critical Race Theory," *Washington Post*, June 19, 2021.

Newberg, Andrew and Waldman, Mark. *How God Changes Your Brain*. New York: Ballantine Books, 2009.

Niebuhr, Reinhold. *Justice & Mercy*. Edited by Ursula Niebuhr. Louisville, KY: Westminster/ John Knox, 1974.

_____. *Moral Man and Immoral Society*. New York: Charles Scribner's Sons, 1932.

_____. *Reinhold Niebuhr: theologian of public life*. Edited by Larry Rasmussen. Minneapolis: Fortress Press, 1991.

Nieman, Donald. *Promises to Keep: African-Ameriacns and the Constitutional Order, 1776 to the Present*. New York and Oxford: Oxford University Press, 1991.

Noble, Safiya. *Algorithms of Oppression: How Search Engines Reinforce Racism*. New York: NYU Press, 2018.

Obama, Barack. *The Audacity of Hope*. New York: Crown Publishers, 2006.

Otis, James. *Rights of the British Colonies Asserted and Preserved*, 1764.

Pager, Devah and Quillian, Lincoln. "Walking the Talk? What Employers Say Versus What They Do." *American Sociological Review* 70, No.3 [June 2005]: 355-380.

Paradise, Brandon. "How Critical Race Theory Marginalizes the African-American Christian Tradition." *Michigan Journal of Race and Law* 20. 2014: 116ff.

Pelagius. Letter to Demetrias. 413.

Peller, Gary. "Race-Consciousness," *Duke Law Journal* (1990).

_____. Telephone interview. Jan. 26, 2023.

Pluckrose, Helen and Lindsay, James. *Cynical Theories: How Activist Scholarship Made Everything About Race, Gender, and Identity – and Why This Harms Everybody*. Durham, NC: Pitchstone Publishing, 2020.

Posner, Richard. *The Problems of Jurisprudence*. Cambridge, MA: Harvard University Press, 1990.

Ray, Victor. *On Critical Race Theory: Why It Matters & Why You Should Care*. New York: Random House, 2022.

Reid, Thomas, *Essays on the Intellectual Powers of Man.* 1785. Edited by A. D. Woozley. London, 1941.

_____. *Essays on the Active Powers of Man.* 1786.

_____. Letter to Dr. James Gregory. 1788.

_____. Letter to Lord Kames. 1775.

_____. *Practical Ethics.* 1751ff. Edited by Knud Haakonssen. Princeton, NJ: Princeton University Press, 1990.

_____. *On the Argument from Prescience against Liberty.* n.d.

Roberts, Dorothy. "The Meaning of Blacks' Fidelity to the Constitution." *Faculty Scholarship at Penn Law* 293 (1997): 1761-1771.

_____. "Punishing Drug Addicts Who Have Babies: Women of Color, Equality, and the Right of Privacy." *Harvard Law Review* 1419. 1991.

Robinson, David. *Slavery in the Structure of American Politics, 1765-1820.* New York: Norton, 1979.

Rossano, Matt. *Supernatural Selection: How Religion Evolved.* London and New York: Oxford University Press, 2010.

Schaeffer, Richard, editor. *Encyclopedia of Race, Ethnicity and Society*, Vol. 1. Abingdon: Routledge, 2003.

Sherry, Susanna and Farber, Daniel. *Beyond All Reason: The Radical Assault on Truth in American Law.* New York and London: Oxford University Press, 1997.

Smith, Page. *The Constitution: A Documentary and Narrative History.* New York: Morrow Quill, 1980.

Spivey, Michael. *Who You Are: The Science of Connectedness.* Cambridge, MA: MIT Press, 2020.

Stephens, Greg, Silbert, Lauren, and Hasson, Uri. "Speaker-listener neural coupling underlies successful communication." *Proceedings of the National Academy of Sciences* 2010:14425-14430.

Stewart, Dugald. *Elements of the Philosophy of the Human Mind.* 1792/1814. Boston: James Munroe, 1843.

Swain, Carol. "Critical Race Theory and Christian Education." *Be the People News*, January 15 2020.

_____. "Critical Race Theory is Rooted in Cultural Marxism." *Be the People News*, January 22 2020.

_____. "Does Progress Require Shaming and Embarrassing Our Children?" *Be the People News*, January 9, 2020.

_____. and Schorr, Christopher Jr. *Black Eye for America: How Critical Race Theory Is Burning Down the House.* n.p.: Be the People Books. 2021.

Tenesa, Albert, Navarro, Paul, et al. "Recent Human Effective Population Size Estimated from Linkage Disequilibrium." *Genome Research* 2007: 520-526.

Tertullian. *On Exhortation To Chastity.* Ca.204.

Theissen, Marc A. "Opinion: The danger of critical race theory." *The Washington Post.* November 11, 2021.

The United States Sentencing Commission. "Demographic Differences in Sentencing." 2017.

Vaught, Russell. Memorandum for the President, 2020, at https://www.white ouse.gov/wp-content/uploads/2020/09/M-20-34.pdf.

Wade, Nicholas. *The Faith Instinct.* New York: Pantheon Books, 2009.

Ward, Benedicta, Trans. *The Sayings of the Desert Fathers.* Kalamazoo, MI: Cistercian Fathers, 1975.

Washington, George. Circular Letter, 1783.

_____. Letter to Gouverneur Morris, 1786.

West, Cornel. "The Prophetic Tradition in Afro-America." *Drew Gateway* 55, No.2/3. Winter 1984-Spr 1985: 97-108.

West, Thomas G. *Vindicating the Founders: Race, Sex, Class, and Justice in the Origins of America.* Lanham, MD and New York: Rowman & Littlefield, 1997.

Williams, Patricia. "Metro Broadcasting Inc. v. FCC Regrouping in Singular Times." *Harvard Law Review.* 1986: 140ff.

Williams, Robert A. Jr. "Taking Rights Aggressively: The Perils and Promise of Critical Legal Theory for Peoples of Color." *Minnesota Journal of Law & Inequality* 5, No.1. March 1987).

Wills, Gary. *Inventing America: Jefferson's Declaration of Independence.* New York: Vintage, 1979.

Wilson, David. *The View of Life: Completing the Darwinian Revolution.* New York: Pantheon Books, 2019.

Witherspoon, John. *Lectures On Moral Philosophy.* 1774. An Annotated Version, Edited by Jack Scott. Newark, DE: University of Delaware Press, 1982.

_____. *The Works of John Witherspoon.* Philadelphia: William W. Woodard, 1802.

_____. *The Works of John Witherspoon.* Edinburgh: J. Ogle, 1815.

Woodall, James and Ellingsen, Mark. *Wired For Racism? How Evolution and Faith Move Us to Challenge Racial Idolatry.* Hyde Park, NY: New City Press, 2022.

Index